50

KIBBUTZ STUDIES

KIBBUTZ STUDIES

A Digest of Books and Articles on the

Kibbutz

by Social Scientists, Educators, and Others

by

A. I. RABIN

Michigan State University Press

CONTENTS

PREFACE

From time to time I receive inquiries, from students and professional workers as well as laymen, concerning available publications on the Kibbutz. The volume of such requests has increased since the publication of my book on *Growing-Up in the Kibbutz*. The material presented here is a response to future inquiries.

At first, a bibliography only was contemplated. However, after some reflection, I thought that brief resumes to accompany the bibliographic citations would be of further help. They may aid the reader in selecting the references which he wants to examine in greater detail and, possibly, whet his appetite for other items which from the title may only appear to be marginal to his interests.

During the past two decades, interest in Kibbutz society and subculture has been increasing. Descriptive accounts of various of the Kibbutz have been published for years; however, systematic studies and research reports of the economic, social, psychological, educational, and cultural characteristics of the Kibbutz have been appearing only in recent years. The present work is an attempt to gather these items, published in several languages, in one volume. This is, of course, a bibliography and a digest and not a comprehensive review of the literature.

No attempt was made to present an exhaustive or "complete" bibliography. Several criteria governed the selection of the nearly 120 items discussed in this volume. *First,* and foremost, was the intent to include as many works as could be located by social scientists who present either empirical findings or systematic analyses regarding the Kibbutz. *Second,* sources available in English and other European languages were stressed, although not exclusively. *Third,* some Hebrew works of a more fundamental nature were also summarized. *Fourth,* a few authoritative general works and reviews of a broader perspective were included. Finally, my own bias and interest in social, cultural and psychological variables is undoubtedly reflected.

In general, it should also be stated that references to works that make a contribution not only to the understanding of the Kibbutz, but to the respective disciplines of the authors, were particularly favored. In a broader sense, some of the ideas and principles that may be gleaned as contributions to understanding and innovation in our own volatile society were highlighted. An attempt in this direction was also made in the Introduction (Section I).

The classification of the summaries into several sections is somewhat arbitrary. There is a good deal of overlap between economic and social studies, between sociological and psychological reports etc. The reader should be aware that this ordering is not ironclad. To a degree, it reflects and is due to the fractionation of the several disciplines represented.

Finally, it is a pleasure to express my thanks to a number of people who helped in the preparation of this volume. Mrs. H. Morishige, Mrs. E. Studiger, and Mrs. J. Thomas compensated for my linguistic deficiencies; G. Levin and M. Rosner were helpful in calling my attention to elusive bibliographic items; and Dr. J.R.P. French, Jr. encouraged me by seeing the potential usefulness of the work.

A. RABIN
Risskov, Denmark
February, 1971

KIBBUTZ STUDIES

INTRODUCTION

From time immemorial man has been striving to improve his lot upon this earth. Despite many promises that religion has offered of a life hereafter for a glorious future after death, man has been concerned with life before death as well. He has been attempting to fashion a life that will satisfy his basic needs and at the same time adhere to the tenets of morality and justice. This morality has inevitably involved the relationships with his fellow men, the interaction with them, and the development of those cooperative social patterns essential for dealing with the forces of nature and harnessing them for the benefit of the community.

Yet history gives a sorry account of man's efforts to achieve a long-range and continuous state of peace and cooperation. Events over long periods of time illustrate the obverse of morality and cooperativeness. A miserable record exists of wars and persecutions, battles and pogroms, murders and pillage, pointing to man's cruelty to man, to his inability to cooperate with his fellow men in complete peace and harmony. Nations, societies, and communities have fashioned laws and legal systems as well as apparatus for their enforcement, in order to regulate and minimize the violence and cruelty which fill the pages of history. That we have not been altogether successful in our attempts at regulation of man's antisocial behavior is obvious from the numerous failures on the international, national, communal and personal levels. Wars between nations, violence within nations, and crime and suicide continue to plague humanity.

It must be admitted that much of the struggle was, and still is, due to differences in religion, ideology and beliefs. But a good deal of it has sprung from greed and selfishness, from the desire to accumulate wealth and to deprive others from enjoying worldly goods. There has been an evolving, constant struggle between the "haves" and "have nots," between the exploiters and the exploited. Nations, tribes, communities, and individuals have fought for the control of land, goods, and wealth. They have had difficulties in the orderly and just allocation of resources to all members of societies and to all member nations of the world community. Similarly, within the national societies and communities, gross inequalities in earning, wealth, and standard of living have developed and have given rise to various sporadic and spontaneous outbursts on the part of the poor and dispossessed. These discrepancies and inequalities which have precipitated violent tremors within various communities throughout history culminated in the French revolution of the 18th century, the Russian and Chinese revolutions in the present century, as well as other revolutions in many other parts of the globe. There is much seething, underneath relative calm, in Latin America, Africa and Asia. According to various observers, revolutionary eruptions in these various lands are only a matter of time, for the ingredients are there and the measures for the prevention of violence and revolution are much too inadequate and ineffective to prevent what seems to be the inevitable.

Many thoughtful, often religious men, with a keen sense of social justice and morality, have attempted to create and fashion new models of social organization. These models were to be based on cooperation rather than competition, on principles of morality rather than legality, on love and altruism rather than on hatred and egotism. The Essenes and the early Christians exemplify this trend, albeit a short-lived one. These early experiments were based on economic and social collectivism, on cooperation and mutual aid, on the principle of communal rather than private property. They were tiny islands within the seas of larger societies that did not take to them too kindly. They escaped from the mainstream of the national life, thus depriving themselves of any broader influence upon the larger society, and gradually disappeared.

Throughout the subsequent centuries various blueprints have been drawn (such as Thomas More's *Utopia*) for different societies, since the existing ones continued to be unsatis-

2

factory. Actual experiments in the United States and abroad have been undertaken in forming new communities based on collectivism and cooperation, on public ownership of wealth and upon the elimination of private property as the source of inequality and economic and social injustice. Most of those communities, many of which were based on religious principles and dogma, have disappeared after relatively short periods of existence. The major exception, perhaps, are the Hutterite communities in the United States and Canada.

There are many reasons for the failure of the numerous attempts to establish these Utopian communities. Several major ones will be considered. In the first place, some of the communities disbanded because of the members' inability to relinquish completely the mode of life they acquired in early childhood and young adulthood. They found it extremely difficult to give up private property and share equally with fellow members of the collective. "Human nature" in the form of selfishness, individualism, the need for personal possessions and the accumulation of wealth and power asserted itself. The interpersonal conflicts that resulted were the seeds of destruction of the communal enterprise.

Second, the religious dogma of some of the communities included the principle of celibacy. Thus, the communities lasted through the lifetime of the founders. But their religious ideology contained the seeds of communal destruction, for a new generation that might perpetuate the effort was not raised.

Third, even without the handicap of celibacy, other communities were unable to influence or persuade their offspring, the second generation, to follow in their footsteps. "Outside" influences were much too strong. The larger society presented too many glittering aspects for the younger generation. The children of the founders were not prepared psychologically, emotionally, or ideologically to resist the attractions that the larger community held out for them. They were seduced by these incentives and left the communities, which were thus inevitably dissolved.

3

There are many other reasons for the failure of socialistic communities and Utopian experiments. But the ones enumerated are the cardinal ones, for they point out the elements of discontinuity that were a part of their brief existence. Their inability to raise a generation that would perpetuate the ideals and the efforts of the founders led to their demise. Such has not been the case with the Kvutzot and Kibbutzim that were established in Palestine, later Israel, beginning with the second decade of the twentieth century. After about sixty years of the Kibbutz movement and after gradual increase and development, they have proved to be a viable force and continue their existence even today. The 230 Kibbutzim flourish; many with second and third generation descendants of the original pioneers and founders. Wherein lies the success of the Kibbutz, the "Venture in Utopia" as Spiro called it, or "the experiment that did not fail" which is the description that Martin Buber gave it? There are a number of answers that should be given to this question. The answer is not simple; it is complex and multi-faceted. What follows below is a brief attempt to sketch the causes of the vitality and viability of the Kibbutz phenomenon with major stress on Kibbutz education or "collective education."

Viewed superficially and cross-sectionally, the Kibbutz society or Kibbutz subculture does not differ markedly from the socialistic experiments of yore. The Kibbutz is essentially a small "island" within a larger society, the major characteristics of which are that of an enlightened capitalist society. It is similar to some of the nineteenth century communities in the United States; they too were tiny islands of socialism and social and economic collectivism in the broader sea of the competitive capitalist economy, culture, and society in which "rugged individualism," the accomplishments of the person by himself, were stressed and glorified. However, the similarity between the two does not go much further once the historical antecedents and the longitudinal view in the development of the Kibbutz movement are taken into account.

Past communal and socialistic experiments, especially of

nineteenth century America, were undertaken in the context of an already existing society and nation. The patterns of economic and social life had already been fairly well set and solidified. A government, constitution and laws, predominant Anglo-Saxon protestant traditions, have given the country a certain form and a set of values. Also, despite the ideal of equality of opportunity, a certain pattern of social stratification had developed even though fluidity and social mobility have been dominant trends. Hence, the arrival of the social and economic experimenters upon the scene has not been viewed kindly or with a great deal of enthusiasm. The founders of the communal societies and their followers have been viewed with suspicion and derision by the "outside" world, by the vast majority. They have been seen as freaks and queers, if not dangerous anarchists, who were a menace to the continued existence and well-being of the American republic and the American Way of Life. The near-persecutory attitude and the suspicion with which the Hutterite colonies are viewed by some of their neighbors to date are quite characteristic of the past century as well. Thus, these "islands" have been isolated not only by their characteristics, that is by being different, but by the attitudes of a surrounding, relatively hostile and rejecting environment.

Historically, this situation has not been the case with the Israeli Kibbutzim. These collective communities were started by pioneers at the very inception of a new country and a new nation. They did not plant themselves in an existing and relatively stable and constructed society; they started at the very beginning of the process and participated in the *process of constructing* the society, country, and nation. Their ability to withstand hardships in conquering the wilderness and warding off the attacks of unfriendly Bedouins and Arabs gained for them the respect of the rest of the budding nation, the colonists, and townspeople alike. Their persistence in the agricultural enterprise and the resulting rate of productivity further enhanced their position. The intelligence and steadfastness they exhibited in the stubborn pursuit of their economic and social ideals gained for them a position of leadership in the developing country. Thus, a relatively small minority has developed a position of an elite in the country, and leadership markedly beyond its proportionate representation in the population. It was primarily the persistent idealism, physical and moral courage, and clearly developed ideologies that earned for them the enviable position they occupied by the end of World War II and at the outbreak of the war of independence. Then too, the position of the Kibbutzim as paramilitary organizations of a high level of devotion and efficiency further enhanced their status and influence.

The Kibbutz movement, therefore, was in the vanguard of a newly emerging nation, in the forefront of the battles for the assurance of its existence. This fact is in marked contrast to the nineteenth century Utopian communities that came to nations already in existence and created obscure little islands, little eddies against the main social and economic current of the nation as a whole. These communities have not aided in creating the nation; their very existence was rather a criticism of its order and its forms of life and development.

Another important aspect underlying the vitality and viability of the Kibbutz is that it developed a network, or federations of a number of settlements, thus avoiding the social, political, and economic isolation that it would otherwise have suffered and which it would have found difficult if not impossible to endure. The emergence of Kibbutz federations with central planning, coordinating, and governing bodies in such a variety of fields as politics, economics, education, engineering and agriculture, has been extremely important in the perpetuation of the Kibbutz and its continued existence. The formation of a subculture in the physical sense obviated the feeling of isolation: the evolvement of an ideology, life style, and a philosophy of life—the center of which involves collectivism—further strengthened the Kibbutz psychologically and aided its members in their facing and interacting with the external world.

6

This brings us to another important factor—the Kibbutz childrearing and educational system called "collective education." To a large extent collective education has reared new generations that are ready and able to take over, develop, and perpetuate the undertakings of their elders, the pioneers and the veterans. It is also this revolutionary system of childrearing that has attracted the attention of educators throughout the Western world and has intrigued and challenged investigators and researchers in such disciplines as anthropology, psychology, sociology, and others.

A detailed description and presentation of collective education in the present context is not our purpose. However, an attempt will be made to draw the picture in bold brush strokes and stress the most salient aspects of the educational system.

Most significant in the Kibbutz setting is the change in family structure and the important changes in the roles of parents in relation to their children. The entire process of collective education stems basically from this major social reform. Although the family continues to exist, many of its traditional characteristics have been altered or eliminated. First, the family as a physical or geographically located unit no longer exists. From birth to maturity, the child does not reside in the same residence as his parents or his other biological siblings; he resides in one of the units of the children's house or in one of the dormitories of the adolescent society. Secondly, the child's economic dependence upon the parents is eliminated. The child "belongs" to the Kibbutz. A Kibbutz member speaks of "our children," referring to all children born in the Kibbutz, not only to the ones born out of his own union. The Kibbutz often views itself as one large "family" that is responsible for and responsive to all its members. Third, it involves the parents' relinquishment of their traditional role as "socializers" of the child. In the conventional family setting the parents, and especially the mother, is the primary "teacher" of the child in the sense that she shows him how to eat, keep clean, and control his aggression; she

(a) usually applies the appropriate sanctions provided by the culture (rewards and punishment) in an attempt to direct the child's behavior, and she often uses the giving of love or its deprivation as the means of controling of the child. To a lesser extent, the father is a socializer in the typical nuclear family as we know it; he too applies sanctions, or sanctions are applied in his name; he also serves as a model, as does the mother, as a transmitter of the values of the larger society and culture. The parents, in psychoanalytic terms, are the sources of superego formation. Related to these facts is the child's strong emotional relation and frequent dependency upon the parents. Due to the special arrangements in the Kibbutz, these conditions do not prevail. Along with the lack of economic dependency of the child upon his parents, there is a reduced emotional dependency. The socializing of the child is distributed among the several metaplot that care for him during infancy and early childhood as well as among members of the peer group that increasingly become important figures in the life of the growing child. It has also been pointed out that the parents, although they have given up their roles as controllers of behavior and as punishers, to a great extent retain the role of rewarders. The daily afternoon and evening hours, as well as the longer periods on weekends and holidays, are times when the parents are almost completely and uninterruptedly available to their children. They do not need to feed them, direct them, or punish them. They merely want to be with them, give them things, and love them. Thus, these periods are characterized by a minimum of ambivalence and by a maximum of positive interaction. This relationship has sometimes been likened to that of the relationship between grandparents and grandchildren.

The several differences in family structure and parental functions detailed above are but a few of the ones that could be enumerated. However, they are some of the most salient ones, and from the viewpoint of dynamic psychology, among the most important in their effects upon later personality development. Personality of Kibbutz children has been de-

8

scribed in some instances on the basis of clinical, intuitive, and impressionistic observations, and in others on the basis of more systematic data and detailed scrutiny.

In closing this general introductory chapter concerning the Kibbutz movement it may be well to point out several of the special innovations and achievements of the Kibbutz enterprise. In many ways these present a challenge to our own society, which is seeking new ways of dealing with a multitude of social, economic, educational, and community problems. What appears below is a brief list of accomplishments of the Kibbutz movement. The list could be extended, but these are some of the major items that sketch broadly the cardinal characteristics of this Utopian experiment:

(1) the success and efficiency of a non-competitive and cooperative economy based on voluntarism and egalitarianism;

(2) a social structure involving "direct democracy"—decision-making by the entire adult community with little delegation of authority in the decision-making process;

(3) radical changes in the foundations of the family and its structure—the family having no economic function and its child rearing obligations markedly reduced, the major basis for the family being the affectional relationship patterns and emotional ties between its members;

(4) maximization of peer influence in the moral development of children in the Kibbutz setting;

(5) healthy personality development and psychological maturity of children raised under conditions of multiple mothering, development of leadership qualities and good ego strength in functioning under stress.

(6) maintenance of pioneering values from generation to generation.

Finally it should be stressed that total transplantation of the Kibbutz model to other societies would be a questionable enterprise. However, what is fascinating to many, is the possible applications of some of the Kibbutz experience. The challenge is in re-thinking and reevaluating some of our cherished notions concerning community structure, human relationships, economics, and childrearing. The following pages present numerous examples of the problems and concerns of the Kibbutz movement itself. It is hoped that in the process of getting acquainted with these, we may gain further insights into the human condition.

II   GENERAL WORKS

Andersen, B. *Kibbutz* **(Danish). Aalborg, Denmark: Fremads Fokusbøger, 1966.**

In a little over 100 pages this Danish journalist describes a number of social and educational aspects of Kibbutz life, and offers his impressions of the Kibbutz, based on a year's stay in Israel. This publication also contains some photographs, general information about several Kibbutz federations, and a limited (non-technical) bibliography of some dozen items.

Darin-Drabkin, H. *The Other Society.* **New York: Harcourt, Brace and World, Inc., 1963.**

One of the best and most comprehensive presentations on the Kibbutz, especially its social and economic aspects, may be found in this book, originally published in Hebrew by an Israeli economist. After a brief section on communes in general and their history in various parts of the world, the author concentrates on various aspects of Kibbutz life. In his own words: "The main part of the book comprises four sections. The first is mainly descriptive, depicting the day-to-day mechanism of the economic and social activity of the Kibbutz: The organization of production; the planning of work, consumption and the democratic basis of the Kibbutz; economic planning; collective education; the relationship between the collective and its members; the family; etc." The second part deals with "the economic efficiency of the Kibbutz—its achievements in productivity, production, and the standard of living, and its ability to cope with the difficult problems of finance and profitability." Part three and four cover the relationship of the Kibbutz with the outside society and "the specific contribution made by the Kibbutz towards the solution of the problems of modern society."

The contribution is not viewed in "macro-sociological" terms (policy and planning on a large scale), but on the "micro-sociological" level—i.e. the organization of the basic social cell. "The Kibbutz points a way towards higher productivity of labor without recourse to differentiation in incomes and the standard of living. It also shows how real democracy and autonomy can be maintained within the limits of the economic framework, and how the problems of rural settlement in modern society can be solved."

A fairly extensive bibliography stressing economic and organizational aspects is appended. References in education, psychology, etc. are of a relatively non-technical nature and of less recent vintage.

Gjessing, Gutrom. *Kibbutz - non-communistic communism.* **Oslo: Pax Forlag A/S, 1967 (Norwegian).**

This brief volume (of 119 pages) was written "before, during and after the 'weekend' war." The first four chapters present some historical background material and describe the current status of the Kibbutz movement within the broader context of the Israeli nation. In the remaining six chapters, primarily intra-organizational problems of the Kibbutz system are of concern. In addition, brief discussions of Kibbutz economics, upbringing of children, education and the cultural life are offered. Some comparisons between the Kibbutz and other forms of communal life, past and present (e.g. Kolhoz) are made, and the future possibilities of the Kibbutz movement are examined.

The author spent some time in many Kibbutzim, but espe-

12

cially in Yad Mordechai where he had close contacts with some members.

Golan, S. *Studies of the Kibbut.* (Hebrew.) **Tel Aviv: Sifriyat Poalim, 1961.**

In this second volume of Golan's collected works the editors have included mostly essays that are concerned with the broader social structure aspects of Kibbutz society and with its adult world. Interpersonal relations in the Kibbutz, the "generation gap," problems of aging, the problem of the woman, and similar issues are addressed in the first part. This is followed by a detailed treatment of the problems of the family in the modern world in general, and of the Kibbutz family in particular. Concerns of youth in the Kibbutz and issues relating the continuation of the Kibbutz enterprise by the new generations are focused upon in the remainder of the volume.

From the start, the question is raised about the possible effects and effectiveness of changed conditions upon man and changes in his personality. Golan concludes that "the establishment of interpersonal relations based on cooperation, equality and identity of interests of the individual and the collectivity to the point that they become a part of the Kibbutznik's character is a long process, indeed, and cannot be accomplished in one generation; but it is possible to make advances."

He is also concerned with the continuity of the Kibbutz, with the identification of the younger generation with the enterprise which is also viewed as a cell of a future society. However, the problem of aging members brings about the generation gap, but beyond it certain undesirable attitudes to the aged. He advocates educational procedures in providing the "correct attitude" to aging in Kibbutz society.

13

The analysis concerning the status of women brings him to three major recommendations of a programmatic nature:

1. improvement of the woman's working conditions and her professional preparation,
2. lightening the work-load by shortening the work-day,
3. the organization of independent action on the part of women in the struggle for their interest and in the activation of their public power and assurance of their representation in the movement.

In connection with the Kibbutz family, stress is placed upon the general reintegration of the family on the basis of the emotional, personal, and erotic-sexual contacts between the partners. The traditional foundations will no longer do. The new integration has the possibilities for greater stability, but, again, the deepening educational process for family living is imperative. Similar, broader trends in the family throughout the world are also noted.

A variety of topics dealing with youth and adolescence constitute the remainder of the book. In a sense Golan returns to educational issues—primarily those issues connected with raising a new generation whose values will represent continuity in Kibbutz ideology and achievement. There is stress on the need for the Kibbutz society to nurture the collectivistic consciousness of the younger membership. For the Kibbutz to be perpetuated it is essential that its members live in awareness that they want Kibbutz life and in the knowledge of the differences between it and conventional capitalistic society; also, that they know the weaknesses and sources of danger, internal as well as external.

Leon, D. The Kibbutz—*A Portrait from Within*. Tel Aviv: "Israel Horizons" and World Hashomer Hatzaiz, 1964.

Quite appropriately, the author identifies himself in the preface as a member of a Kibbutz of the Kibbutz Artzi federation, which is the largest in the Kibbutz movement. This small book presents a description of the Kibbutzim and the federation and "does not pretend to be 'objective'. . . . It is written from the inside, by one who is totally involved in, and concerned about its struggles, its achievements, and its problems."

In this slender volume, Part One, called "Foundations," offers a concise statement of the historical, ideological, and political background of the Kibbutz movement, with special attention to the Kibbutz Artzi leftist orientation. The bulk of the volume, "How it works" (Part Two), consists of twelve chapters covering a wide range of topics—socioeconomic and political aspects, management, the educational and childrearing system, woman's place in the Kibbutz, and the new generation. Special stress is placed on a discussion of the possibility of creating a "new man" in a new society and on the Hashomer Hatzaiz youth movement which furnished the human element of the Kibbutz Artzi and continues to operate in a parallel fashion to the more formal educational system.

In the concluding part ("Perspectives") the author undertakes an overview of the effects of achievement of statehood in Israel and is critical of the high degree of professionalization and social polarization in the country and of many economic policies of the Mapai-dominated government. He points to the maintenance of the radical traditions by the Kibbutz movement; and to its mission and importance in the country.

Several brief, but useful, statistical appendices (Kibbutz population and distribution of membership, etc.) may be found at the end of the book.

Spiro, M. E. *Kibbutz—Venture in Utopia.* **Cambridge, Mass: Harvard University Press, 1956.**

This anthropological case study is based on field work done in one Kibbutz for a period of about ten months. The book presents a detailed description of Kibbutz life. Following a historical introduction of the Kibbutz and the "moral postulates of Kibbutz culture" the author discusses the European origins of its members, the economy and governance of the communal society, as well as the educational, social and political aspects of the community. The last section (not counting the Epilogue) is devoted to a discussion of "The crisis in the Kibbutz." He concerns himself with intra-Kibbutz tensions such as result from lack of privacy and many other minor and major dissatisfactions that cause members to leave the Kibbutz or, if they remain members, to spend much time in occupation on the "outside." Problems of status involving the mature versus the young, and especially the dissatisfaction of women, are particularly stressed. Both problems are analyzed in some detail in relation to the unique family structure in the Kibbutz setting.

III REVIEWS AND HISTORICAL PERSPECTIVES

Ben-David, J. The Kibbutz and the Moshav. Ch. IV in J. Ben-David (Ed.), *Agricultural Planning and Village Community in Israel.* Paris: UNESCO, 1964.

A comparison of the Kibbutz and Moshav and a historical survey of their origins are offered in this brief chapter. Some statistics concerning the growth of the Kibbutz and Moshav movements since the 1920's are also presented. Between 1922 and 1945 the Kibbutz movement appeared to be the fastest growing (proportionately speaking, in terms of population and numbers of villages) form of settlement in Israel (then Palestine). The pioneering service performed by the Kibbutzim was widely recognized and their influence as an elite group in the new state is manifested by the relatively high number of deputies and ministers with which they are represented. Tabular material on this point is also presented. The several Kibbutz federations are described and the factors determining unique aspects of individual Kibbutzim (such as size, economy, etc.) are also discussed. Finally, the author concerns himself with the internal aspects of the Kibbutz and its future. He feels "that neither family autonomy nor division of labour are necessarily disruptive . . . of the Kibbutz." According to him "The real problem of the Kibbutz does not lie in the autonomy of the family or in the feasibility of maintaining equality among its members, but in the threat to its pioneering and missionary functions." (Apparently the conditions in the early 1960's did not demand pioneering zeal.)

Buber, M. *Paths in Utopia.* **Boston: Beacon Press, 1958.**
(Originally published in 1949.)

At the conclusion of a treatise on socialism and various Utopian schemes attempting to realize socialistic ideals, Buber discusses the Kibbutzim as "an experiment that did not fail." He states: "As I see history and the present there is only one all-out effort to create a Full Co-operative which justifies our speaking of success in a socialistic sense, and that is the Jewish Village Commune, in its various forms." He further points out that the primary ingredient of success was work rather than ideology and considers this "bold undertaking" as a signal non-failure. He does not quite use the word success because for that to occur, "much has still to be done."

Diamond, S. Kibbutz and Shtetl: the history of an idea.
Social Problems, **1957, 5: 71–99.**

Although the author states that this essay is based on data (interviews, projective techniques, etc.), none are presented in a systematic fashion. He attempts to pull together and integrate his observations as a participant observer in a Kvutzah (a small Kibbutz) by means of a "functional-historical" analysis of the Kibbutz movement. His major thesis is that the Kibbutz represents an over-reaction of its founders, and an antithesis to their life in the "Shtetl" (small Eastern European town). Many of the ideological principles, family life, and childrearing seem to stem from this attitude. Such values as pioneering, equality, asceticism, and other values are viewed in the light of the major thesis: over-reaction to the Shtetl.

The author sees the Kibbutz in a state of crisis since the "vatikim" (veterans) are tired and interpersonal tensions seem to focus attention upon the discrepancy between ideology and reality.

Diamond, S. The Kibbutz: utopia in crisis. *Dissent,* 1957, 4: 132–140.

Concerned with "crisis" as involved in ideology (hired labor) and interpersonal relationships ("over-collectivization and the role of women"). Primarily a polemic article.

Friedmann, G. The Kibbutz adventure and the challenge of the century. *Revue francaise de sociologie* (French), 1964, 5: 259–289.

In this broad survey of the Kibbutz history, demography, economics, democracy, family structure, and education, the author identifies the "lights and shadows." Following his analysis he stresses the more positive aspects of the Kibbutz contribution, with special emphasis upon the human element and the quality of the Kibbutz membership and its ideology.

Infield, H. F. *Cooperative Communities at Work.* New York: The Dryden Press, 1945.

Only one chapter in this book entitled "The Kvutzah" (ch. IX) directly concerns communal settlements in Israel. Most of the volume is devoted to descriptions of a variety of communal settings throughout the world (e.g., Hutterites, Kolhoz, etc.). Chapter IX traces the origins of the Kvutzah (or Kibbutz), discusses some of the social and childrearing aspects during the early years, and reports selected statistical data on the economics of a group of the early settlements during the 1930's.

A wide range of topics are briefly treated in this chapter in addition to those mentioned above. The management, economic basis, conditions of work, social cooperation, and the achievements of the Kvutza are considered. Finally, a comparison between the Kvutza and other cooperative forms of settlement (smallholders) is also drawn.

Rabin, A. I. Of dreams and reality: Kibbutz children.
Children, **1969, 16 (4): 160–162.**

A review essay of Bettelheim's book *The Children of the Dream* (1969). The author is critical of the nature of Bettelheim's evidence and questions especially his conclusions regarding "the leveling effect" of Kibbutz education (with respect to school achievement), speculations regarding the alleged incapacity for intimacy, emotional "flatness" and lack of responsiveness, lack of flexibility and of independent action, and repressed sexuality on the part of the Kibbutz-reared adolescent and adult. There are also comments concerning the applicability of Kibbutz childrearing principles and procedures to the American scene.

The author further questions Bettelheim's notions regarding a "simplified superego" in the Kibbutz-reared individual and points to reasons for greater complexity.

"Despite these handicaps" it is felt that the book "may serve as a rich source of hypotheses for future systematic investigations into personality development in the Kibbutz."

Rabkin, L. Y. A very special education: the Israeli Kibbutz. *Journal of Special Education*, 1968, 2: 251–261.

In addition to a review of past research and a description of Kibbutz education, the author briefly outlines the concerns of his own project. This study was undertaken as a followup of Spiro's work in Kiryat Yedidim which was carried out in 1951–1952. The research involves personality development in children who are "currently residing in Kiryat Yedidim," the majority of whom are the offspring of the subjects of the previous study (Spiro's). The study is both nomothetic and idiographic. Some problems which were not considered by Spiro but are examined in this project are: intellectual development and functioning (findings appear to be at variance with Rabin's results), family relationships and their perception by children and adults, the effects of the first Kibbutz-reared generation upon their offspring, and the differences between them. This is a broad outline of the questions raised. Results of the research on these issues are yet to be reported.

Rabkin, L. Y., and Rabkin, Karen. Children of the Kibbutz. *Psychology Today*, 1969, 3 (4): 40–46.

A general descriptive overview of Kibbutz childrearing and a discussion of some of the published research findings. Also included are some comments regarding the applicability of the Kibbutz experience to the American scene.

21

Schwartz, R. D. Behavior research in collective settlements in Israel. *American Journal of Orthopsychiatry,* **1958, 28: 572–576.**

This discussion of doing research in the Kibbutz covers some issues of strategy in addition to the danger of bias affecting the results. In order to make a more objective evaluation of Kibbutz society the traditional ethnographic procedures are not sufficient; there may be a tendency to see in the Kibbutz a substitution of social for economic inequality based on Western-oriented values. The author proposes the use of comparison; e.g. comparison of the Kibbutz with the Moshav, not with American or Western society. Also, the use of quantitative techniques is particularly valuable in comparison and in the maintenance of objectivity.

Skard, T. Collective childrearing in practice. (Norwegian.) *Norsk Pedagogisk Tidsskrift,* **1963, 47: 87–109.**

Essentially, this is a fairly comprehensive and integrative review of the relevant systematic research published in English. Special stress is laid on the analysis and conclusions stemming from the work of Rabin and Spiro. Personality characteristics, positive and negative, are described and the emphasis is laid upon the opportunities for further research in this "laboratory," which is constantly changing. An appendix includes the methods of investigation and the numbers of subjects in the more systematic investigations.

Skard, T. Kibbutz children. (Norwegian.) *Norsk Pedagogisk Tidsskrift,* **1967, 51: 111–122.**

This article contains an up-to-date review of several general books on the Kibbutz (Leon, Darin-Drabkin) and several psychological and sociological publications mainly concerned with childrearing, along with some abstracts of presentations at a 1963 conference in Oranim, Israel.

Stern, B. *The Kibbutz that was.* **Washington, D.C.: Public Affairs Press, 1965.**

Although this publication is primarily concerned "with the economic and political functions of the Kibbutz as an integrated entity operating within the large institutional framework of the State of Israel," part of it also deals with issues of education and training (especially ch. VIII). The latter is, however, only a brief description of the system. The final chapter following one titled "Changes and Rumblings," is concerned with the future of the Kibbutz, its possible expanding influence and the limitations on such a possibility. Central to the entire volume, however, is the consideration of the effects of expanding industrialization on the Kibbutz —its social structure, interpersonal relations, ideology, and institutions.

IV   IDEOLOGICAL AND POLITICAL ISSUES

Arian, A. *Ideological Change in Israel.* **Cleveland: The Press of Case Western Reserve University, 1968.**

Of main concern to the author of the monograph is the nature of ideological change in Israel, especially among two elite-groups: public servants and university students. The two are considered to represent present and future political leadership of the country.

Following a theoretical analysis of ideologies, their relationship to political parties and their activities in Israel, there is a report of interview data with the two Israeli samples that deal primarily with economics and foreign policy issues. Then, two chapters are devoted to the "Kibbutz movement" and "The Kibbutz Ideology." On the basis of the available literature, the author identified ten "elements of Kibbutz ideology" which were used as the basis for an interview schedule. These elements are:

(1) Complete mutual responsibility according to the principle, "From each according to his ability, to each according to his needs" (cooperation);

(2) "Establishment of society without any differences in privilege or material possession" (equality);

(3) Abolition of private ownership of the means of production;

(4) Character is formed by society which stands above the individual;

(5) "The image of the Jews must be that of a laboring nation";

(6) "The realization of the principles of Kibbutz ideology must take place within an agricultural framework";

(7) "The Jews of the world constitute a nationality and not only a religion";

(8) "The Jews of the world should immigrate to Israel";

(9) "Those Jews in the diaspora who are at the summit of the economic pyramid must form its base in Israel"; and
(10) "Kibbutz values should be accepted as the values of all mankind."

Since Kibbutz ideology has been central in Israel policies and since the author has been primarily concerned with the hypothesis of "ideological decline," this schedule of ten elements and a paralled schedule of "personal-practice" were administered. The "Kibbutz ideology" schedule was presented three times—present evaluation of each element, past (ten to fifteen years earlier) evaluation, and an evaluation of public acceptance and utility of the several elements.

Among the public servants who constituted nearly half of the 233 person sample were two subgroups: Knesset members and senior civil servants. Among these were Kibbutz members, former Kibbutz members, and those who were never Kibbutz members.

The general conclusion is that the data support the hypothesis of ideological decline. This statement, however, is qualified in that "The ideology as a systematic set of ideas remained vital; the intensity of acceptance has declined." Additional results invokes the point that "former Kibbutz members experience more ideological change—and in the direction unfavorable to the ideology—than present members or those never associated with the Kibbutz."

The author further concludes that Kibbutz ideology remains politically viable and that "there is no reason to suppose that the Kibbutz movement will decline in political strength or economic importance in Israel."

Cohen, E. *A comparative study of political institutions of collective settlements in Israel.* **Jerusalem: Hebrew University, 1968 (Mimeo).**

There seems to be considerable interest, outside as well as inside the Kibbutz movement itself, in the adequacy of the functioning of "the purest democracy in the world." This is one of several studies concerned with the broad base of participatory democracy which characterizes the management and government of the Kibbutzim.

Veteran ("mature") Kibbutzim are the subject of this study and the focal problem is "whether the system of direct democracy is capable of functioning satisfactorily in such Kibbutzim, and what problems of growth and increasing complexity pose to this system." The following areas of behavior, opinions, and attitudes were investigated:

1. participation of the membership in voluntary activities (work and official roles),
2. extent of participation in the public meetings of the Kibbutz,
3. opinions concerning the role and functions of the general meetings,
4. opinions about the major institutions of the Kibbutz,
5. opinions regarding the formation of elites, and
6. "attitudes toward Kibbutz democracy."

One veteran Kibbutz from each of three federations—Kibbutz Artzi, Kibbutz Meuchad, and the religious federation—served as settings for the research. The full (adult) membership in the Kibbutzim ranged from 238 to 437. Total samples were polled on some of the issues and twenty-five percent representative samples were employed in the case of others. Methodology and procedures are not detailed in this publication, although there is a profusion of tabular material presented.

The general finding "is that in the Kibbutzim under study,

growth and complexity did *not* essentially impair the workings of Kibbutz democracy." With respect to the specific questions investigated (listed above), some relevant conclusions are listed below.

It seems "that between 1/3-2/5 of members of the Kibbutzim under study performed some kind of responsible project within the last five years." Yet many of these roles were on a relatively low level. The problem of lack of involvement of the majority of the membership is discussed.

Participation in the communal assemblies (general meetings) is quite high. In one kibbutz (Kibbutz Artzi) about 2/5 of the membership participated in all five consecutive assemblies sampled; only 1/5 did not participate in any of them. Similar, but somewhat lower, participation was found in the other Kibbutzim. Participation of women was consistently lower than participation on the part of men.

There was generally satisfaction with the functions of the general assembly, although there were marked differences between the Kibbutzim in this respect.

A high degree of satisfaction with some Kibbutz institutions was expressed (secretariat and work committee), while a large degree of dissatisfaction with others (e.g., "committee on social questions") was also indicated.

There is a fairly general feeling, especially in the largest Kibbutz (of the Kibbutz Meuchad), that the "Kibbutz is in the process of developing a political elite." This feeling is present to a lesser degree in the Kibbutzim that have a broader base of membership participation in public roles and functions.

Overall, the attitude toward Kibbutz democracy was quite affirmative—"the members themselves expressed satisfaction with the workings of the system in most of its respects."

In addition to important differences with respect to the democratic institutions and degrees of satisfaction with them in the three Kibbutzim (due to historical, ideological, and structural differences) a number of problem areas are discussed. The high degree of passivity among many members,

27

especially women, and their lack of attachment to communal institutions is a major issue. Also the lack of involvement and the "relative passivity of the second generation is an ominous sign for the future of Kibbutz democracy."

Despite these and a number of other lacunae pointed out by the author, he concludes with a conditionally optimistic sentence: "We thus proved that direct democracy does not necessarily deteriorate under modern conditions of growth and complexity, though it may be threatened by these conditions." He adds further that "in order to preserve it, the Kibbutz will have to develop ways and means to combat both the functional difficulties which democracy faces nowadays, as well as the growing passivity and lack of concern of members with democratic institutions."

Rosner, M. Direct Democracy in the Kibbutz. *New Outlook*, **1965, 8:29–41.**

Kibbutz democracy is described as based on the principles of *voluntary* affiliation of the membership, on *cooperation* via active participation of most members in Kibbutz functions, and on *egalitarianism* due to the desire of the Kibbutz to achieve equality in all areas of life. Cooperation and egalitarianism, especially in the decision-making processes are not readily attained, but must be actively pursued. Kibbutz democracy functions via the (1) general meeting of the membership, (2) organizational structure such as committees and coordinators, and (3) the different types of participation of all members in making the Kibbutz work.

The author reports numerical data on membership participation in the general meetings (50–55 percent on the average) and on the broad participation of the membership in the various coordinating and managerial tasks of the Kibbutz economy, cultural and educational activities, and social life.

There is a considerable "changeover" rate despite the increasing demands of specialization in various posts.

The article concludes with these observations:

(1) There is no clear tendency of decline in the function of the general meeting as a main agent of democracy despite the increase of size of the Kibbutz and the "greater distance of members from policy-making centers."

(2) The great amount of interaction of members in many areas of life maintains the authority of the general meeting ("town hall").

Sarell, M. "Conservatism" and "innovation" in the second generation in the Kibbutzim. (Hebrew.) *Megamot*, 1961, 11: 99–123.

Several hundred young men and women (ages: 17–40) born in the Kibbutz were asked a series of questions designed to assess the extent of their adherence to the original Kibbutz ideology (conservatism) or the extent to which they deviate from it and favor new patterns (innovation). A sample of over 400 "first generation" members was included for comparative purposes. The investigation was conducted within the framework of the Ichud federation of Kibbutzim and is based on interview and questionnaire data combined with other sources of information. The sources are not entirely clear from the tabular material presented.

Four areas were the focus of concern as the possible indices of "conservatism" or its opposite: *family* (attitude to sleeping arrangements for children, size of family, supper in the individual apartment, parents' influence in the occupational placement of children), *consumption* (attitudes to simplicity and standard of living, to investment vs. consumption, and public consumption vs. private, etc.), *work* (generational allocation to the various branches, work satisfaction and its causes, etc.), and other special issues of particular concern to the second generation (army, studies, etc.).

Response data revealed a variety of patterns related to specific issues and no clear-cut conclusion regarding the position of the second generation along the conservatism-innovation dimension. With respect to such issues as communal (non-family) sleeping arrangements for children, opposition to having supper in private quarters and to possession of personal items from non-Kibbutz sources, the younger generation is more conservative than the first generation which reflects more compromises with the original ideology in their responses. In the same vein, the younger generation is also opposed to parents taking a role in determining the occupation of their children. On the other hand, the younger generation is less conservative in its attitudes to asceticism in consumption (values held by the older generation). A number of other differences of smaller magnitude appear. Especially interesting are the differences between a younger group of the second generation (17–18-year olds) and the older group; the younger, due to their more recent contact with the Kibbutz educational system and ideological indoctrination, tend to be more "conservative," more satisfied with work and interested in agriculture, than the older segment of the second generation.

It is difficult to come to a general conclusion regarding a "generation gap" in this group of Kibbutzim, especially since a number of the comments and observations are related to data not included in this paper, but in other (footnoted) reports.

Schwartz, R.D. **Democracy and collectivism in the Kibbutz.** *Social Problems,* 1957, 5: 137–147.

In this essay, the main concern is with an analysis of the relationship between economic collectivism and democracy. In comparing a Kvutzah and a Moshav, the author concludes that the Kvutzah is at least as democratic as the Moshav. He sees, however, some assertion of managerial power in the Kvutzah and sees in its possible increase a danger to democracy. Concerning the more theoretical issue, the conclusion is that "democracy *can* exist in a collective society." But, he feels that there is no support for Lenin's view that "collectivism necessarily produces a greater degree of democracy."

Talmon-Garber, Y. and Stop, Z. **Asceticism—patterns of ideological change.** In *"Sefer Bussel"* (Hebrew). Tel-Aviv:Bialik Institute 1960, pp. 149–189.

Secular asceticism, in contradistinction to the religious asceticism which characterizes the protestant ethics, has been one of the important principles of Kibbutz ideology. However, changes in the ideology have been taking place as a result of external influences and internal stresses and adjustments. The authors distinguish four different patterns in the attitudes of over 400 interviewees of twelve Ichud Kibbutzim. The patterns are as follows: the ascetic pattern, the cultural-stylistic, the situational, and the consumer pattern. The first pattern stands for the continued acceptance of the traditional ascetic values of the pioneering Kibbutz movement. Proponents of the consumer pattern are on the opposite end—rejecting the ascetic values altogether. The cultural-stylistic pattern advocates simplicity as a style of life, but not extreme self-denial or asceticism. And, finally, the situational pattern refers to the necessity to economize, depending on the balance between income and consumption; economizing may be a necessary evil, depending on conditions, but not for its own sake. The two latter patterns are viewed as compromise patterns between the conservative (ascetic) and the innovative (consumption pattern) extremes.

The two extreme patterns were represented almost to the same extent in the interviewed population—one third in each category. The remaining third was evenly divided between the two compromise patterns.

Contrary to expectations, there was little difference between different types of Kibbutzim, whether of recent vintage or of veteran status. The newer Kibbutzniks' ideology is similar to that of the old timers.

V ECONOMICS, MANAGEMENT, AND AGRICULTURE

Frank, M. *Cooperative Land Settlements in Israel and their Relevance to African Countries.* Basel & Tuebingen: Kyklos-Verlag and J. C. B. Mohr, 1968.

One chapter in this study of cooperative agriculture in Israel and its application to the "third world" in Africa south of the Sahara is devoted to an analysis of Kibbutz agriculture and economics. Although the author is critical of the excessively democratic structure of the Kibbutz and sees its procedures as too complicated and "economically detrimental to the settlement," he also is aware of many of its advantages. It is his view that the Kibbutz pattern of economy solves a number of problems of village economics and public life. Large scale operation based on "rational" functioning and efficiency maximizing productivity rates, combination of agricultural and non-agricultural enterprises, and sources of income, and the good standards of cultural and public services that reduce the attractiveness of urban centers, are seen as the advantages of the Kibbutz pattern. However, the author does not see this model as appropriate for the developing African countries because of its dependence upon certain "socio-ideological" principles which would not be acceptable to the peasantry concerned. Instead, he sees other forms of cooperative farming and economy, also developed in Israel, as more suitable for African agriculture. He also views the Israeli experience and expertise as an important source of assistance in planning and organization which has been tapped to some extent and may be used even more extensively in the future.

Kanovsky, E. *The Economy of the Isaraeli Kibbutz.*
Harvard Middle Eastern Monographs, XIII. Cambridge,
Massachusetts: Harvard University Press, 1966.

Following a general survey of Israeli agriculture, in the
first chapter of this monograph, a second chapter concerned
with the "historical and institutional background of the Kibbutzim" is presented. It is in Chapter III that the author
deals more directly with the Kibbutz economy—with factors
of production (land, labor, and capital) and with finances
(income and expenditures). Some detailed tabular material
on the distribution of the labor force in the various branches
of the economy, investment in agriculture, and value of
agricultural production (in 1960) are presented.

The next three chapters, which constitute the bulk of the
volume, concern themselves with "the changing position of
the Kibbutzim in the national economy" and with the efficiency, productivity, and profitability of the Kibbutz
economy. Considerable statistical data are presented in these
chapters and in the appendix of the book.

In keeping with the national trend, there is an increasing
stress on non-agricultural undertakings in the Kibbutz
economy. However, the data indicate a high rate of growth
of agricultural productivity in the Kibbutzim during the
period of 1949–1960—"an annual (compounded) rate of
growth of 15.8 percent in agricultural output; 2.1 percent
in the agricultural labor force; and 11.5 percent in fixed
reproducible agricultural assets." These figures are considerably higher than in non-Kibbutz agriculture in Israel. One
study quoted indicates that between 1953 to 1958 the
Kibbutz agricultural worker produced between 69 to 119
percent more than the non-Kibbutz (Jewish) agricultural
worker.

In discussing the "profitability" of Kibbutz economy it
appears that "the Kibbutzim *as a whole* suffered net losses
(or net dissaving) during the period 1954 to 1960, and then
showed net profits in 1961 and 1962. There is a more consis-

tent tendency for the older, more established, Kibbutzim to show profit than loss.

The general conclusion regarding the deficits is that the consumption (living standards) of the Kibbutz had risen considerably—beyond the level of production (which has also risen) and consequently deficits were inevitable.

In the concluding chapter (summary and conclusions) the author offers a number of reasons and points to external and internal factors that affect profitability in the Kibbutzim. Among the former are such factors as short-term high-interest loans taken by the Kibbutzim, higher security and marketing costs in many Kibbutzim in outlying parts of the country, subsidies granted to branches popular in non-Kibbutz agriculture, etc. The internal factors are several, such as a diversified economy which is often less profitable, opposition to the use of hired labor, consumption branches requiring a high proportion of labor days, and the standard of living in the Kibbutzim has been largely divorced from the current profitability, cost of political and other activities, etc.

Finally, the author concerns himself with the future of the Kibbutz movement, which of course depends much on the new generation of Kibbutz-reared young men and women. He sees, essentially, a very slow rate of increase in the Kibbutzim, but its proportion in the Israeli population will continue to decline, barring a large influx of new recruits which is not expected.

Kugel, Y. Communalism, Individualism, and Psychological Modernity: A Comparison of Kibbutz and Moshav Members on the Overall Modernity and Dogmatism Scales. Unpublished doctoral dissertation, Michigan State University, East Lansing, 1970.

Starting with the observation that Kibbutz social structure "is relatively traditionalistic" (according to conventional modernization theory) yet recognizing that its factories are highly efficient (compared with urban factory productivity) and modern, the author wonders how modern Kibbutz members are psychologically.

The Overall Modernity Scale and the Dogmatism Scale were given to fifty-three members of a Kibbutz and to 104 members of three different Moshavism. Although the Moshav members scored higher on the Modernity Scale, the differences were not statistically significant. However, "Kibbutz members scored significantly lower (more modern) on the Dogmatism Scale items."

A general conclusion of this study is that "psychological modernity" can be present in "a traditionalistic social structure"; one, apparently, does not dictate the other.

Orbach, E. *Cooperative Organization in Israel—The Kibbutz and the Moshav.* **Madison, Wisconsin: Center for the Study of Productivity Motivation, 1968.**

Of major concern to the author of this slim volume is the organization and productivity of the Israeli collective (Kibbutz) and cooperative (Moshav) settlements. Primarily based on data previously published, the study emphasizes the rapid growth of economic productivity, especially in the Kibbutz. "The purpose of this short book is to raise the interest of management theorists in the organizational forms of both." It is the contention of the author that the organization and operation of Kibbutzim and Moshavism support modern management theories (e.g. McGregor's "y" theory, Likert's "participation" theory and Maslow's "Synergy" theory). He further suggests that the organizational forms of these types of settlement may be useful in the agricultural and industrial development of underdeveloped countries. At any rate, research on the management of the Kibbutz and the Moshav is considered worthwhile and potentially useful in the facilitation of economic growth.

Pallman, M. *The Kibbutz—the structural transformation of a concrete type of commune in a non-socialistic environment.* **(German.). Tuebingen: Kyklos-Verlag Basel, 1966.**

This is a detailed socio-economic study of the Israeli Kibbutz. Two chapters (three and four) are devoted to a detailed description of two contrasting types of Kibbutzim—a primarily industrial Kibbutz (Dalia) and a primarily agricultural one (Reshafin).

A conceptual analysis of the Kibbutz, detailed in the first chapter, divides the "social sphere within which all human relations are enacted . . . into a 'business' hemisphere and a 'habitat' hemisphere." The former involves transactions outside the Kibbutz, while the latter refers to all other relations (accommodation and consumption, education, and leisure). Within the two hemispheres, collectivism in relation to degrees of private-public property is considered. The second chapter presents a brief historical survey of the development of the Kibbutz movement and other cooperative ventures in Israel. The fifth and last chapter, entitled "The Israeli commune in a critical developmental phase," deals with a variety of economic and social topics. Regional cooperative industrial planning looms large. Considering personal autonomy and family relations, the author feels that the family and procreation has "not reduced in any appreciable measure the special bonds of solidarity between Kibbutz members."

Rosner, M. Social aspects of industrialization in the Kibbutz. Paper presented at the International Symposium on "The role of group action in the industrialization of rural areas" Tel-Aviv: International Research Center on Rural Cooperative Communities, 1969 (Mimeo).

After presenting an analysis of the necessary social conditions for industrialization, including characteristics of individuals and the nature of the social system, the author concludes the paper with two major points.

"1. The special way of the Kibbutz in establishment of industrial enterprises within a village, as a single ecological unit, points to the possibility of avoiding the negative results of the process of industrialization, that went usually together with leaving of the village by young, vigorous people, destruction of social frames and phenomena of alienation and anomie. The establishment of industrial enterprises within the Kibbutz becomes a stabilizing factor, enlarging the possibilities of employment, variegating the courses of individual development and thus strengthening the social structure.

"2. In the collectivistic (communal) framework of the Kibbutz, the disconnection is avoided between the ownership and the work, which is one of the phenomena usually going with the industrialization of the village. As opposed to the transformation of an independent farmer into a hired worker, with all the change of social status implied, the cooperative-collectivistic industrialization enables the preservation of the worker's feeling of independence within the democratic framework of management of the enterprise and his participation in the decisions."

Talmon-Garber, Y., and Cohen, E. **Collective settlements in the Negev. Ch. V in J. Ben-David (ed.),** *Agricultural Planning and Village Community in Israel.* **Paris: UNESCO, 1964.**

The Kibbutz movement has, to a degree, retained its pioneering role by settling, and continuing to settle, the arid zones of the Negev. This, despite the fact that "75 per cent of all settlements founded in the Negev in the post-State period are Moshavim."

The pioneering functions of the Kibbutzim are viewed—
1. as a spearhead in developing the outlying arid regions via long periods of preparation and hard work,
2. as "long term experimentation and careful planning and flexibility . . . before economic activity can be conducted on a more entrepeneurial basis," and
3. as defensive military outposts for the protection of the borders and more vulnerable settlements.

Most of this essay is devoted to an analysis of the status of the Kibbutz movement and the modes of its participation in the development of the Negev. "The crisis of recruitment" of new members for the Kibbutzim from the Israel's youth (there being no longer a significant immigration from Central or Eastern Europe) and its implications are discussed at length. Also treated are the two major patterns of assistance to developing Kibbutzim in the Negev. "Federal assistance" refers to the help given by the several federations to its member Kibbutzim. "Regional cooperation" refers to the mutual assistance between Kibbutzim in a certain area, regardless of their affiliation (federation or political party). The differences between the two methods are also analyzed. According to the author "Federal schemes are essentially defense mechanisms which protect the Kibbutzim from outside pressures and enable them to conserve their ideology and institutional structure." On the other hand, regional cooperation is "more flexible and change-oriented" and tries to deal with newly developing trends adaptively. Some accommoda-

39

tion between the two patterns results, and the emergence of a young new elite "critical of the established leadership of the federations" is also seen.

Vallier, I. Structural differentiation, production imperatives and communal norms: The Kibbutz in crisis. *Social Forces*, **1961–1962, 40: 233–242.**

"Mayeem Kareem" (fictitious name), and its 160 adult members, is the primary setting where the alleged 'Kibbutz crisis' was studied by the sociologist-investigator and author of this article. The study attempts to learn something about the "crisis" at "two levels of social structure: a level between the Kibbutzim and wider society and a level between one Kibbutz and its several subsystems."

After a brief historical review of the changes in Israel since the establishment of the state and the different demands and pressures made upon the Kibbutzim, the author concerns himself with sources of tension (assignment of jobs, decision making, elitism, formal communication techniques, etc.). He offers "a sociological interpretation of the crisis."

The interpretation consists mainly in pointing out that the economic (external) demands require a complex division of labor. "The intensity and scope of the total production operation are forcing changes in the structure of power . . . organization of work . . . role system." The consequences are developments toward formality, hierarchy, specialization, etc. which tend to break down the informal communication patterns.

A major conclusion offered is that "the Kibbutzim's complex internal strains are closely related to the incongruence between the communal norms governing the Kibbutzim and their functional position in a wider society." It might be added, parenthetically, that this conclusion is not self-evident, nor overwhelmingly supported.

VI   SOCIOLOGICAL FACTORS AND THE FAMILY

Cohen, E. Progress and community: Value dilemnas in the collective movement. *International Review of Community Development,* **1966: 15–16, 3–17.**

Following an analysis of the technological and economic advances in the Kibbutz, the author concludes that there is a basic conflict between two sets of values: "progress and communality." He notes that as a consequence "The Kibbutz gradually loses its *Gemeinschaft* character and becomes a *Gesellschaft.*"

The Kibbutz is viewed as a combination of "primitivity" in social structure and "modernity" in its technological and economic organization. Viewing the future, the author feels that "the tragedy of its situation seems that it cannot preserve its 'communality' without restricting the very dynamism of its development." The problem is identified, but future developments are not predicted since a reversal of the trend may depend on such factors as the degree of affluence, attitudes among the second and third generation, and other unpredictables.

Etzioni, A. Solidaric work groups in collective settlements. *Human Organization,* **1957, 16: 2–6.**

An attempt is made "to explain the wide differences in solidarity observed in work-groups" in two Kibbutzim. On the basis of responses to fifty-one questions concerning work relations and attitudes and from "information gathered through observation," several indices of solidarity were formulated:

1. Degree of consensus of group members with Kibbutz production policy and with regard to work
2. Extent of "we" feeling
3. Relations between members (positive, neutral, negative)
4. "Subjective estimates of . . . mutual aid in the group."

The situation in 14 work-groups was evaluated and the relationship between group solidarity and degree of segregation from the Kibbutz is highlighted. The highest degree of solidarity was found in the group of one Kibbutz in charge of farm crops (falha); next highest was a parallel group in the second Kibbutz, "The lowest is kitchen in both Kibbutzim". Child care groups occupy an intermediate position with respect to solidarity. The author also points out that the highest solidarity is found in groups involved in "production" and this work is also most prestigious; kitchen work is lowest in prestige, is not segregated (constantly open to members' criticism), and the relevant groups seem to show least solidarity. The question as to why segregated work-groups who maintain solidarity are also conforming, rather than deviant, is yet to be answered.

Etzioni, A. The functional differentiation of elites in the Kibbutz. *American Journal of Sociology,* **1959, 64: 476–487.**

Development of differentiation of roles and emergence of elites is traced in the Kibbutz, from its beginning as a nucleus (Garin) of recruits from youth movements to the stage of becoming an "older" Kibbutz. According to the author four types of elite emerge (expert, managerial, social, and cultural). First, there is differentiation at the "role level and later on the personnel level." Furthermore, "a hierarchy of elites tends to develop in which specialized elites are at the bottom, dual elites at the middle level, and collectively-oriented elites at the top." The results of the analyses are considered to be consonant with predictions from Parsons' theory.

Gerson, M. On the stability of the family in the Kibbutz (Hebrew). *Megamot*, **1966, 14: 395–408.**

Starting with Burgess' description of the modern family as one of "partnership," rather than an institution, the author points out the similarity of the Kibbutz family in the areas of economics, childrearing, and interpersonal relationships. He sees in the Kibbutz family a more extreme development of the partnership trend because it is not an economic unit, professionals participate (with parents) in the education of the children, and there is a sharing in home responsibilities and decision making. The Kibbutz family is viewed as based mostly on affectional and emotional ties. The question of its stability is raised and studied by means of a survey of the incidence of divorce in 142 Kibbutzim, encompassing more than 10,000 families. Data are reported separately for veteran Kibbutz members and for the younger sector (including those members born in the Kibbutz). The percentages of divorces in the older and younger groups were *ten* and *six* respectively. The divorce rate (annual) for the Kibbutzim seems to be lower than for other Israeli families (based on census figures 1958–1961). The author concludes that the Kibbutz marriages are quite stable; more than in the modern family in Israel. Also, this is relatively remarkable since, because of economic and other reasons, it is more difficult to decide upon a divorce outside the Kibbutz, especially when children are involved.

Raven, B.H., and Leff, W.F. The effects of partner's behavior and culture upon strategy in a two-person game. In *Studies in psychology* **(Rifka R. Eifermann, ed.),** *Scripta Hierosolymitana,* **1965, 14: 148–165.**

Two groups of high school students, equally divided between the Kibbutz Artzi (great emphasis on collective ideology) and the Ihud (moderate collective ideology), totalling 114 were administered a "two-person non-zero-sum game" which is designed to measure the degree of cooperativeness of the subjects. One third of the S's faced "a partner who played a consistently non-cooperative game," and another third faced an unconditionally cooperative partner; still another third had a "conditionally cooperative" partner, but the results of this group did not differ from those of the unconditionally cooperative conditions. Included were also 24 young American subjects who were preparing to spend a few months in Kibbutzim.

The results indicated, contrary to expectations, that "difference in Kibbutz ideology did not significantly affect cooperation in the game. Kibbutz youth tended to follow an essentially competitive strategy, in varying degrees, in response to each type of partner, suggesting that they tended to see this as a game rather than try for the best absolute score." The American youth, however, showed "a predominance of cooperation, given a cooperative partner."

Rettig, S. Relation of social systems to intergenerational changes in moral attitudes. *Journal of Personality and Social Psychology,* **1966, 4: 409–414.**

Moral attitudes (obtained by means of a questionnaire that presents fifty different ethically disputable behaviors) across three generations of Kibbutz and Moshava (ordinary village) subjects totaling 883 were compared. From the vantage point of socio-cultural theory it was predicted that intergenerational changes in the Kibbutz will be larger, despite the greater cohesion among its members, "because of its replacement of the kinship system by an age-group system for the transmission of attitudes." Following a factor analysis of the results "for consensual validation," "a multiple discriminant analysis for assessment of overall distances between groups" and "a multivariate analysis of variance for measurement of separate interaction effects on each factor," it was concluded that "intergenerational changes in the Kibbutz were greater on two dimensions, religio-family and affluence." The results are interpreted as supporting sociocultural theory of attitude change.

Rosenfeld, Eva. Social stratification in a "classless"
society. *American Sociological Review,* **1951, 16: 766–774**

Despite political and economic democracy, the author sees the emergence of social stratification, of high and low status, in Kibbutz society; she is particularly concerned with the process of emergence of social strata and the role they play in the process of social change. There developed a group of leaders who are in actuality managers of enterprises for which they are responsible. These "managers-leaders" can see the effects and products of their work, whereas the work of the rank-and-file seems to be submerged into anonymity. There is a certain attitude of deference, especially on the part of newcomers, to the leaders. The author also sees different roles of the two strata in institutional change. The managers-leaders try to encourage greater productivity and austerity in consumption, while the rank-and-file presses for a higher standard of living. Several methods of blocking change by the managers are also discussed.

Rosenfeld, Eva. Institutional change in the Kibbutz.
Social Problems, **1957, 5: 110–136.**

In this sociological analysis of change in Kibbutz institutions, the author focuses on one aspect of consumption, that of clothing. The work is based on a field study via participant observation and intensive interviewing in thirteen Kibbutzim (of the three major federations). The major question raised is: "why should the original institutions not continue to function smoothly and efficiently?" With respect to the distribution of clothing by the Kibbutz central authority, two sources of tension and pressure have developed. First there was a shift in motivation "from a comparatively monolithic system of common goals" to more diversified personal goals (e.g. higher standard of living, greater freedom in selecting goods to suit one's tastes, etc.). Second, inadequate socialization of members in their social roles and inadequate control of deviant behavior. The shift in motivation is explained on the basis of the change in the prestige of the Kibbutz and consequent values in identifying with it. Also "natural" differentiation of interests and values and achievement of financial security furthered the change in motivation and a move away from austerity. The second aspect was due to inexperience and a rejection of formalization which would destroy the image of the Kibbutz as a "big family." The difficulties in distribution of clothing brought about two changes—a "private account" system, leaving decisions of clothing to the individual; and the raising of the standard of consumption, formalizing members' rights and imposing sanctions on deviant behavior.

Rosenfeld, Eva. The American Social Scientist in Israel: case study in role conflict. *American Journal of Orthopsychiatry*, 1958, 28: 563–571.

Social scientists in their role as participant observers in the Kibbutz expose themselves to unique conflicts which may threaten the objectivity of their endeavor. In addition to the usual sources of bias, guilt and anxiety in the social scientist may be an important source of selective perception and consequent distortion. The sources of the investigator's inner conflicts are feelings of loss of identity ("who am I? a scientist or a member of this community?") and "of standing on the brink of commitment, involvement, total identification" which are in opposition to the role of the objective observer. Possibilities of "negative bias" as a result of protective devices needed to maintain a separate identity in the investigation are also noted. The paper concludes with "several requirements" for behavioral research in the Kibbutz, concern with function as well as dysfunction of individuals and the entire group, critieria for the assessment of morale and well being, and attention to the several developmental stages of childhood.

Schwartz, R.D. Social factors in the development of legal control: a case study of two Israeli settlements. *Yale Law Journal*, 1954–53, 63: 471–491.

In an effort to study the effects of economic collectivism upon the relationship between legal and informal controls, the *Kvutza* (Kibbutz) and the *Moshav* are comparatively examined. The community as a whole exercises controls and administers sanction in case of the former, whereas a special committee or tribunal operates in the latter type of settlement. Stress is laid, and some supportive data reported, upon the greater importance of public opinion in the Kibbutz, as compared with the Moshav, and its influence in controlling behavior. The development of an effective informal control system is seen as a "partial explanation of the failure of the Kvutza to develop a legal control system." The Moshav failed to develop an informal control system, hence the development of legal institutions. The explicitness of behavioral norms developed in the Kvutza, in contradistinction to the Moshav, are also considered in some detail.

Sheffer, J. *The reflection of children's sleeping arrangements in the social structure of the Kibbutz.* **(Hebrew.) Tel Aviv: Ichud Hakvutzot Vehakibbutzim, 1967.**

Two groups of Kibbutzim in which the sleeping arrangements for the children differ were studied in detail by means of a structured interview. Responses of 408 adults in nine Kibbutzim in which the children sleep in the parents' apartment were compared with responses of 410 adults from nine matched Kibbutzim where the "collective" sleeping arrangements (in the childrens' house) were maintained. The effects of these differences upon a wide variety of related attitudes and collectivistic ideology were the primary focus of this carefully designed and executed sociological study.

Although the family is an important social unit in the Kibbutzim that practice both systems, in the Kibbutzim with the family-sleeping arrangements there is greater cohesion among the adult members (couples) in political opinion and action. Women tend to compare themselves, with respect to appearance, to the city woman and housewife. On the other hand, men in the "collective" Kibbutzim tend to be more critical of the current changes in the Kibbutz woman's image and of the greater concern with femininity and personal appearance.

Generally the "family" group tend to be less active in the politics of the Kibbutz and in social affairs than the collective group. Women participate less than men in the general assemblies; this is true of both groups.

With respect to education, the family group has broader authority than in Kibbutzim with the collectivist pattern. In the latter, Kibbutz institutions have greater authority. Women of the collectivist group seem to express greater dissatisfaction with the small degree of authority enjoyed by the family. A minority in both systems wishes to expand the functions of the family in personal budgeting and consumption, with the trend being greater in the family group. Generally the trend is that the expansion of the functions of the family is at the expense of the functions of Kibbutz institutions and is a factor in the greater polarization of the roles of the sexes in the family.

All of the work was done in the Kibbutzim of the "Ichud" movement.

Spiro, M.E. Is the family universal? *American Anthropologist,* **1954, 66: 839–846.**

According to Murdock the following four functions are essential to the definition of the family: sexual, economic, reproductive and educative. When these criteria are applied, the family can be said not to exist in the Kibbutz. Sexual exclusiveness has not been important in Kibbutz unions; rather, psychological intimacy seemed to hold couples together. There is no economic cooperation between couples, for each member maintains his individual status in the Kibbutz; the couple does not divide the household labor, for all labor is done by the Kibbutz. Another important indicator of the Kibbutz system not meeting the criteria for the family is that the physical care and social rearing of the children are not the responsibility of the parents but of the Kibbutz as a whole. The education and socialization of the children are the responsibility of the community as a whole, which assigns nurses and teachers to the children.

The interpretation of Kibbutz life shows that it is the Kibbutz itself which fulfills Murdock's criteria of the family. Due to its dissimilarity, the Kibbutz is not a nuclear family. What this study does suggest is that the Kibbutz can function without the family because it functions as if it, itself, were a family; and it can so function because its members perceive each other as kin, in the psychological implications of the term. Because of their shared experiences and mutual involvement with the Kibbutz, the members of the Kibbutz consider themselves comrades or brothers. This is shown by the low incidence of endogenous marriage. Kibbutz members feel they can't marry someone they grew up with.

The concluding proposition of this study is that although the Kibbutz constitutes an exception to the generalization concerning the universality of the family, structurally viewed, the entire society has actually become a large extended family. This can only work in a society such as the Kibbutz where the members perceive each other psychologically as kin. "Only in a 'familial' society such as the Kibbutz, is it possible to dispense with the family." There must, however, also be a population limit on such a phenomenon.

Spiro, M.E. Marriage . . . in the Kibbutz. *American Anthropologist,* **1854, 56: 840–842.**

Sexual relationship and economic division of labor are the main criteria of the conventional marriage. The economic criterion does not exist in the Kibbutz marriage. "What are the motives for such a union and how does it differ from an ordinary love affair?" are the questions raised.

It is also pointed out that premarital relations are not negatively sanctioned in Kibbutz society, therefore—"If sexual satisfaction may be obtained outside of this union, what is the reason for becoming 'couples'?" Here the author stresses the needs for intimacy—physical as well as psychological. The latter may be expressed by such concepts as "security", "dependency", "succorance" and "comradship".

Talmon, Yonina. **Aging in Israel, a planned society.** *American Journal of Sociology*, **1961**, 67: 286–295.

Despite the fact that the Kibbutzim have solved many problems present in the aging period, a number of areas of strain seem to remain. On the positive side—"Aging members enjoy full economic security. Communal services take care of them in case of ill health or infirmity. Retirement from work is gradual and does not involve an abrupt and complete break from work routines." In addition, aging members continue actively in community life. Participation in community and social affairs provides a substitute for the lost functions. "In many cases it compensates the aging member for his gradual loss of competence and status in the occupational sphere." Most important, according to the author, is the fact that grown-up children are expected to stay in the community which their parents established and thus remain in contact with the parents and offer them some security, much appreciated during the aging period.

According to the analysis presented in this article, there are many sources of strain that interfere with the smooth transition to the status of aged. Some of these sources are the predominantly future-oriented and youth-centered features of Kibbutz society, the great stress on work and productivity, and the fact that the attempt of the older person to hold on to his job often limits the opportunities for the younger generation. This is particularly accentuated in Kibbutzim where there is little distribution according to age and where there are only two generations and no intermediate groups.

In addition to greater community participation as a compensatory activity, "withdrawal from the occupational sphere enhances the importance of the family." There tends to be a greater concentration upon contacts with children and grandchildren which are often based on reciprocal services.

The need for planning retirement, leisure activities, domiciliaries, etc. is stressed and some of the plans are outlined at the end of the report.

Talmon, Y. The family in a revolutionary movement—the case of the Kibbutz in Israel. Ch. 13 in M. Nimkoff. *Comparative family systems.* **Boston: Houghton Mifflin Co., 1964.**

An incisive analysis of the changes in the status of the family in the Kibbutz is presented in this essay. The main focus is upon "the interrelation between changes in communal structure and modification of family organization in a revolutionary and collectivist movement." The author presents an historical overview of the origins of the "antifamilism" in the early years of the Kibbutz movement. She deals with her material on the basis of "the hypothesis that *there is a certain fundamental incompatibility between commitment to a radical revolutionary ideology and intense collective identification on the one hand and family solidarity on the other.*"

Following a survey of the reasons that prompted the young immigrants to establish the Kibbutz form of life in the first place (overreaction to families of origin, hostile environment, reclamation of the land, etc.) and a discussion of the family functions, sexual ethic, roles and relationships within the family, there is a detailed account of the changes that have taken place as a result of increased prosperity, "routinization" processes, economic consolidation and expansion, and the development of intergenerational continuity; the latter tending to replace the discontinuity that characterized the early phases of the Kibbutz movement. Wider kinship ties, greater differentiation of roles, and the strengthening of the family are among the major changes stressed by the author. She concludes that "The antifamilism of the revolutionary phase has thus abated, but has not disappeared altogether. It has been superseded by a moderate collectivism which regards the family as a useful though dangerous ally. The Kibbutzim still try to control and limit the family and direct it towards the attainment of collective goals. The main problem of the Kibbutzim from a dynamic point of view is how to allow the family more privacy and a certain internal autonomy without harming the cohesion of the community."

Talmon, Yonina. **Mate selection in collective settlements.** *American Sociological Review*, **1964, 29: 491–508**

In this article the author presents an interesting sociological and psychological analysis of marriage trends among the second generation in three veteran Kibbutzim. She points out the exclusively "exogamous" marriage patterns among the Kibbutz-born young people. A survey of 125 second generation marriages did not yield *a single case* of marriage between members of the same peer group (Kvutzah). All marriages were outside the group ("exogamous"). Five marriage patterns were identified: 1. *Intra-second generation* (inter-peer group)—only 3%; 2. *Intra-* Kibbutz (new Kibbutz members, not reared in the Kibbutz)—31%; 3. *Inter-* Kibbutz (marriage to members of other Kibbutzim)—23%; 4. *Intra-movement* (marriage to members of the youth movement committed to Kibbutz ideology)—27%; 5. *Extra-movement* (mates selected "outside" of the Kibbutz or its allied movement)—16%.

Although the exogamous patterns are quite obvious they are not seen as an "institutional normative pattern" (as in some other societies), but as an "attitudinal and behavioral trend". The author's analysis directs attention to some of the positive aspects of the middle patterns (2, 3 and 4) which constitute the bulk of the marriages. The "extra second generation" marriages prevent "the emergence and consolidation of large and powerful kinship groupings within the Kibbutz" (which would be inimical to its existence), aid in bridging the "intergeneration cleavage", check the emerging stratification (with the old timers forming an elite), revitalize the relationship between the Kibbutzim and the youth movements, and "bridge the gap between the Kibbutz and other sectors of society". On the negative side, these marriages may threaten Kibbutz continuity. Extra-movement marriages, especially, may lead to desertion of the Kibbutz.

On the more psychological level, the question is posed: "How can we account for this sexual neutralization (among peer group members) on the motivational level?" Here the analysis is informative, but somewhat less satisfactory. The author stresses the constant commitment of the Kibbutz children to the group which discourages "dyadic withdrawal". Personal and intimate relations are established with parents, early in childhood, outside the group. Thus, the exogamous tendency "should be viewed as one manifestation of *the basic distinction between peers who are comrades and intimates who are 'outsiders'.*" Later, the exogamous tendencies in the grown children represent a rebellion against the parents who are interested in the continuity of the Kibbutz and in having them marry within it. The second generation thus combines their "exogamy" with the "endogamy" demanded of them by the parents, and marry within the movement, but not necessarily within the peer group or their own Kibbutz. It "*reconciles dissociation with identification and maintains a flexible balance between rebellion and loyalty."*

A fairly detailed analysis of parent-child relationships, peer relations, and relations between the sexes at different age levels is also included. But, the main point that is stressed is that the "purely interpersonal approach to mate selection" is inadequate. In the non-familistic society of the Kibbutz (where kinship affiliations and institutional regulations of mate selection are not important), the marriage patterns *"mesh closely with the overall institutional structure and serve as crucial integrative mechanisms."*

Talmon-Garber, Y. The family and the children's sleeping arrangements in the Kibbutz. (Hebrew.) *Niv Hakvutzah,* **1959, 8: 19–68.**

In this extensive study of attitudes in twelve Ichud Kibbutzim to the collective sleeping arrangement the memberships were about evenly divided into those who want the children to sleep in the parents' quarters and those who want to maintain the children's house sleeping arrangements. There are considerable variations as to the ages at which parents want their children with them at night, in the reasons given for their demands for a change, or for the maintenance of the status quo, etc.

Talmon-Garber, Y. The family in collective settlements. In *The Third World Congress of Sociology,* **1956, 4: 116–126.**

Effects of transition from "Bund" (characterized by devotion to common cause, collective identification, informality, and homogeneity) to commune (formalization, less intense collective identification, etc.) upon family roles and position in the community is the main subject of this sociological analysis. The non-familistic tendency in the ideology of the collective movement from its inception is analyzed in terms of internal relations in the family, recreation and social relations, and the delegation of most traditionally familial functions to the collective institutions. Marked changes in the position of the family, especially in the older settlements, are detailed by the author who notes that *"The further the collective is from the 'Bund' type, the more marked and far-reaching are changes in this respect"* (family position and organization). The family assumes the position of a "basic social unit" involving intensification of parent-child relationships, strengthening of kinship ties, and greater sex-role differentiation. Many other concessions of the community in the direction of the stronger familistic trend are listed in the article.

Talmon-Garber, Y. The family in Israel. *Marriage and Family Living,* **1954, 16: 343–349.**

In the context of a broader survey of family patterns in Israel during the past World War II period, the author discusses the unique features of the Kibbutz family, especially as a "non-familistic" organization of agricultural production "within a cohesive communal framework." A description of the role patterns of parents vis à vis the children follows. The family has delegated most of its functions and the main stress is upon the affective-personal relation. The creation of families in the Kibbutzim "has weakened the primary group characteristics of the community." The increased tendency for greater autonomy of the family, and privacy, is also stressed. Also some modifications in the children's sleeping arrangements (e.g. in parent's home), in some of the Kibbutzim, briefly illustrate the trend. Some minor demographic trends (lowering of age of marriage, slight increase in fertility rate) are also mentioned.

Talmon-Garber, Y. The family and occupational placement of the second generation in the collectives. (Hebrew.) *Megamot*, 1957, 8: 369–392.

"The purpose of this paper is to analyze the basic principles of the collectivistic pattern and to trace mechanisms conducive to its proper functioning" in the non-familistic occupational placement of growing children. A range from an exclusively collectivistic pattern to a modified pattern based on compromise with the demands of the family is described. Attitudes towards the demands of the family regarding occupational placement is related to its position in the Kibbutz. These attitudes are noted in different types of Kibbutzim where the position of the family varies. Also, women tend to be more familistic than men, and the second generation somewhat more collectivistic than the first. The results summarized above are based on interviews with 415 respondents from twelve Kibbutzim who reacted to the following questions:

A. Is it desirable that the family should influence the vocational choice of its children?
B. Should the Kibbutz consider the demands of the parents in this matter?
C. Should the Kibbutz consider the desire of the children?

The study was conducted in the "Ichud" federation only.

Talmon-Garber, Y. Social change and family structure.
International Social Science Journal, **1963, 14: 468–487.**

Three patterns of family organization—Kibbutz, Moshav and city—are compared with respect to the "impact of radical and rapid social change."

In the Kibbutz, the greater trend toward familism and a gradual development of stronger kinship ties, as opposed to the previous anti-familism, are discussed. The contrast between the "collectivized" family and the urban refugee family is stressed. Whereas the former is involved in "a partial disengagement and emancipation" from the collective, the latter is engaged in a process of reorientation and reengagement with the community. In the Moshav, the kinship unit seems to be an intermediary between the family and the community.

Talmon-Garber, Y. Social structure and family size.
Human Relations, **1959, XII: 121–146.**

A recent increase in fertility rates in the Kibbutzim where they had been below replacement levels is related by the author to ideological changes and consequent changes in the social structure of the Kibbutzim. She notes a marked ideological shift from the "Bund" (homogeneity, devotion to common cause, intense collective identification, etc.) to the "Commune" (differentiation, redefinition and accommodation of collective values, etc.) pattern and classifies the Kibbutzim studied along these dimensions. Long, intensive interviewing of 415 subjects (about ten hours) yielded data regarding attitudes towards family size. Four ideological patterns were discussed: collective-oriented limitation, collective-oriented expansion, family-oriented expansion, and individual-oriented limitation. Generally, the author states:

"We found the tendency of family limitation at the two extremes of a continuum, in extreme collectivism at one end and in extreme individualism at the other, whereas the tendency of family expansion was found to be anchored in moderate collectivism and in familism."

Yamane, T. *Kibbutz: its sociological analysis.* **(Japanese.) Tokyo: 1965.**

Changes in the Kibbutz system and projections with respect to its future as a viable cell in a larger non-collectivist society are of major concern in this sizable volume (817 pages). The author spent some time in Israel and in a Kibbutz as a participant observer. In this book, in addition to drawing on the available literature, he reports his personal observations of the Kibbutz society, its economy, educational system, etc. The volume concludes with an evaluation of the enterprise as a Utopia. He points out some of the shortcomings (e.g. the limited effects upon society of the Kibbutz undertaking) and some of the advantages of Kibbutz society. He also discusses the recent trends of "liberalization" and greater flexibility with respect to collectivism and the regression to individualism on the part of the older members. The future of the Kibbutz is seen as depending upon the extent of the external pressures from the larger society and upon the internal tensions within itself. He quotes from the literature opinions regarding the familistic trends among the older generation, but also notes less dissatisfaction with collectivist values in the second generation. Finally, he concerns himself with the Kibbutz culture and the way it channelizes inborn aggressive drives: "The culture of the Kibbutzim seeks to steer aggressive drives into social channels, and the educational system of the Kibbutz has succeeded in producing individuals who have controlled these impulses."

VII   THE STATUS AND PROBLEMS OF WOMEN IN THE KIBBUTZ

Golan, Y. The woman in the Kibbutz. (Hebrew.)
Hachinuch Hameshutaf, **1962 13: 37–42.**

Woman's problems in the Kibbutz are viewed not as uniquely characteristic of Kibbutz society, but as universal problems of women in the modern world. Kibbutz women's achievement of "full equality in economic and social rights —not only in theory but in practice"—is stressed. However, "we have not reached equality in work." The author presents data which show that the vast majority of women are engaged in service and educational enterprises in the Kibbutz, while men are much more involved in agricultural and other productive enterprises, and in management. She also notes the tendency of women to desire more contacts with their children as an indirect way of broadening the authority of the family. Several suggestions are made for improving the working conditions of women in the Kibbutz and extending the range of their activities.

Rabin, A. I. Kibbutz mothers view "collective education."
American Journal of Orthopsychiatry, **1964, 29: 140–142.**

Interviews with 123 Kibbutz mothers were held in thirteen different Kibbutzim. The interview schedule consisted of twenty-three items concerned with the mothers' attitudes to "collective education." Data on the eighty-one Kibbutz born and forty-two non-Kibbutz born mothers are briefly summarized (non-tabular form). It is concluded that most of the mothers "fully accept collective education," although some minor criticisms and need for reform were voiced. Seventeen percent of the respondents were judged to have negative or ambivalent attitudes, the major problems being concern over insufficient time spent with the child, separation at night, and inadequacies of the metapelet. No marked differences in attitude between the two subgroups were found. A further conclusion: "the need for mothering is, by and large, satisfied under conditions of collective education."

Rabin, A. I. Some sex differences in the attitudes of Kibbutz adolescents. *Israel Annals of Psychiatry and Related Disciplines,* **1968, 6: 62–69.**

"Over 300 Kibbutz-raised 17 and 18 year olds responded to an especially devised 40 item questionnaire and to the Maudsley Personality Inventory. The main purpose was to study sex differences in the attitudes of Kibbutz adolescents. The results indicate the following:

1. Predominant majorities of both sexes are highly satisfied with Kibbutz education and with the communal life in general.

2. Whenever there was dissatisfaction in some area, higher percentages of girls indicated discontent.

3. Foremost in the comparative discontent of the girls were the limitations in occupational scope for women in the Kibbutz, the monotony of the unchangeable educational-social peer group living unit, and the concomittant limitations upon the relationships within the nuclear family.

4. As a group, the girls report themselves as more moody, more anxious, and emotionally sensitive and labile than the boys.

"The discussion of the results yielded a few suggestions for possible reform in the educational structure of the Kibbutz." This project was completed within the framework of the Kibbutz Artzi.

Rabin, A. I. The sexes—ideology and reality in the Israeli Kibbutz. In Seward, G. H., and Williamson, R. C. (eds.), *Sex Roles in Changing Society.* New York: Random House, 1970.

Central to this essay is the issue of the discrepancy between Kibbutz ideology with regard to equality for women and the actual reality as it emerges after some six decades of struggle and adjustment. After a general description of Israeli culture from a broad perspective and the historical background of the Kibbutz movement and its ideology, the author focuses upon "freeing of the woman" as a major, ideological principle. Directly related issues such as the family in the Kibbutz, childrearing procedures, and the sex identification process are discussed in some detail. In connection with the identification process it is noted that male roles are more clearly defined. The boys "learn to want" to occupy the male status as defined in the Kibbutz, but the girls, despite the equality doctrine in the educational system, are influenced by ambivalence of the women toward their roles. Some girls "learn" *not* to "want" the roles that women occupy in their community. Also, "the educational system, although stressing equality, is permeated with traditionally masculine values."

Possible sources of female discontent (which, incidentally, is not strong enough to lead to serious defection or deviation) are noted: 1. "the promised equality of opportunity and freedom of occupational choice never materialized: and 2. many women began to have second thoughts about their 'liberation' from the household, especially from the care of their children. The need to be more with their children has been asserting itself. . . . Counteracting the feminine discontent is the increased amount of time women in Kibbutzim are spending with their offspring."

The final observation is that we may note a gradual accommodation between ideology and factual reality. Ideology tends to be modified in the face of experience, although experience may be directed by ideological principles. Adjustments in the school curriculum "that will prepare women for the kinds of functions they are undertaking anyway and the increase in family-centeredness" are the major aspects of the accommodation.

Rosner, M. Women in the Kibbutz: changing status and concepts. *Asian and African Studies* **(Annual of the Israel Oriental Society). Jerusalem: Israel Oriental Society, 1967, III, 35–68.**

A research project on the status of women in the Kibbutz was carried out in 1965–6. In this partial report on an interview survey of 466 women from twelve Kibbutzim and eighty-six men from four Kibbutzim ("controls"), the focus is upon aspects of the shift from the conception of "mechanical equality" to "qualitative equality" of women. The author distinguishes "three basic patterns" of thought in regard to the issue of equality of women. First is the notion of "natural" differences between the sexes that leads to inequality, a notion opposed by social scientists who stress the social configuration. Second, the "rivalry" between the sexes ends up in man's gaining the upper hand and relegating woman to the secondary position. Third, is the duality of women's roles which blur her "self-identity." This duality interferes with her achievements in careers, etc. and blocks equality. This tripartite orientation was utilized in studying the Kibbutz samples.

Respondents felt that women could do most administrative tasks in the Kibbutz. Typical feminine traits agreed upon by the majority are "the tendency to become emotional, readiness to feel insulted and shyness. Greater concern of women with family was generally noted." In general, there is an egalitarian attitude with respect to skills and abilities and a differential one in the case of social roles and aspira-tions. Ten to thirty percent of the women felt the presence of discrimination in different areas.

As to the contradiction of roles, the author feels that the Kibbutz is placing increasing stress on the family group and that there is a weaker collectivistic orientation. This trend intensifies the problem of the duality of roles. Women want more children, see their role as caring for the family now, are interested in cosmetics, etc.

There is further analysis of data on Kibbutz seniority and sex of respondents. Some differences are reported in tabular form.

Rosner, M. *Changes in the Conception of Equality of Women in the Kibbutz.* **(Hebrew) Givat Haviva, Israel: Institute for Research of Kibbutz Society, 1969.**

"Consistency and inconsistency in the conception of equality of the woman in various areas among members of the Kibbutz Artzi-Hashomer Hatzair" is the subtitle of this monograph. This is a more extensive coverage of related data reported, in part, in the 1967 publication by the same author.

A number of hypotheses, to be gleaned from the summary of the results, were investigated by means of interviews. The interviews were of a total of 560 women and 100 men from different Kibbutzim. The selection of the Kibbutzim was designed, especially, to represent their different ages. Random sampling from the individual Kibbutzim was under-taken.

The detailed results of this complicated investigation are presented in a profusion of tables and diagrammatic material included in the monograph. Some of the major conclusions drawn from the data appear below.

(1) The hypothesis that there is a lack of congruence be-

tween the various components of the ideology regarding the status of the woman in the Kibbutz was confirmed. . . .

(2) The general concepts (images) of the characteristics and abilities of the sexes are most egalitarian (compared with other societies), but the concepts of occupational roles are least egalitarian, while the concepts of public activity occupy a middle position.

(3) The non-egalitarian concepts are especially common in those areas in which the processes of role differentiation according to sex are particularly strong. There is, therefore, a connection between the strength of the processes of differentiation and the extent of egalitarian attitudes.

Incidentally, the notion that the processes of differentiation are particularly strong in the veteran (older) Kibbutzim and that accordingly there is a greater frequency of non-egalitarian concepts in them was not substantiated.

The author sees two possible explanations of the tie between the strength of the differentiation processes and the extent of egalitarianism in attitudes:

(1) Demographic pressures (women bearing children in younger Kibbutzim), changes in work arrangements, and the rise of the familistic trend brought about role differentiation in various areas, which in turn is reflected in the norms and concepts. The differences between the Kibbutzim stem from the differential power of these processes.

(2) From the very beginning there was a difference between the members of the different Kibbutzim in ideological conceptions, and these differences determined the strength of the processes of role differentiation; for instance, the readiness of the women to work in agriculture or to fulfill public "masculine" functions was a determining factor.

It appears to the author, on the basis of the findings, that the first alternative is more reasonable and acceptable.

(1) In the first place, Kibbutz-reared girls who received a most-egalitarian upbringing in Kibbutz educational institutions show that their conception in a number of areas is less egalitarian than that of most of the other women inter-

viewed; there seems to be a drop in the striving for equality in the fulfillment of roles which, apparently, stems from acceptance of reality.

(2) In the younger Kibbutzim the weight of the demographic factor in the differentiation of roles in the occupational area is important and not necessarily a consequence of non-egalitarian technology.

(3) It appears that the greater egalitarian character of the "middle" (aged) Kibbutzim stems from the fact that the two factors pressing toward differentiation—the demographic factor in the young Kibbutzim and the strong familistic orientation in the older Kibbutzim—are relatively weaker in this group of Kibbutzim.

Generally, those interviewed felt that there is greater egalitarianism in the Kibbutz than outside its perimeter. Also, along with the acceptance of a certain role differentiation in the area of work, there was stress on guarding the full equality in the areas of (communal) activity and economic status of the women.

Talmon-Garber, Y. Sex-role differentiation in an equalitarian society. In T.G. Lasswell, J. Burma and S. Aronson (eds.), *Life in Society*. Chicago: Scott, Foresman and Co., 1965.

Changes in the direction of an increase in family functions in the Kibbutz are accompanied by a "concomittant increase in sex-role specialization." This trend is contrary to that evident in the early development in the Kibbutz movement.

Several questions were asked in the course of interviews with more than 300 Kibbutz members. Four classifications of ideological patterns emerged: (a) an "equalitarian" pattern involving strict equality and interchangeability of roles, (b) the "joint" pattern, more flexible and less equalitarian involving some sex-role differentiation, but close cooperation and joint activities of husband and wife, (c) a "differentiated" pattern, not rigid but characterized by a larger number of specialized as compared with shared activities, and (d) a "segregated" pattern which dictates rigid sex-role differentiation. Child care and services are defined as "women's work."

In response to the question about the division of family tasks, the general opinion is distributed mostly along equalitarian and "joint" ideological lines. However, in the specific areas of care of children, care of a flat, and care of clothing, a small minority opted for the equalitarian pattern; sixty-four percent see care of children as a joint activity; in the care of the flat forty-one percent fall into the joint category, and twenty-four percent in the differentiated; seventy percent report the segregated pattern as most appropriate in the care of clothing. Although the ideological pattern with respect to sex-role differentiation in Work Assignment falls heavily in the joint (thirty-eight per cent) and the differentiated (forty-eight per cent) categories, the actual division of labor and participation in committees is even more differentiated and segregated.

The author stresses a growing discrepancy between the professed equalitarian ideology and actual growing role differentiation as a source of strain. She describes, briefly, several institutional mechanisms devised to bridge the gap between ideology and reality. These mechanisms are: rationalization and mechanization of service institutions (women's occupations), professionalization in many of the "feminine" occupations, diversification of feminine occupations, and "de-differentiation" by developing more spheres of joint activity (reducing number of exclusively feminine or masculine occupations).

VIII PSYCHOLOGICAL FACTORS, PERSONALITY, AND MENTAL HEALTH

Amir, Y. The effectiveness of the Kibbutz born soldier in the Israel defense forces. (Hebrew.) *Megamot*, 1967, 15: 250–258 Also in *Human Relations*, 1969, 22: 333–344

Kibbutz-born, "Kibbutz-bred" (spent the years 10–16 in the Kibbutz), and non-Kibbutz ("others") male soldiers, who entered the Israel Defense Forces during the year 1963–64, were compared with respect to "efficiency," personality, and intelligence variables, and on "background" factors. Efficiency was defined on the basis of three criteria—"volunteering for especially difficult and dangerous tasks; advancement in rank and job level; successful completion of courses of military training."

The Kibbutz group was markedly superior to the other groups in intelligence, educational level, knowledge of Hebrew, and personality ratings. The Kibbutz-bred group was superior to "others" in educational level, personality scores, and language knowledge. More than one-third of the Kibbutz-bred and others were of Afro-Asian origin, whereas only four percent of the Kibbutz group had such a background. Markedly higher percentages of Kibbutz born soldiers showed a high frequency of volunteering, were selected for command position, and succeeded in officers school. Kibbutz-bred soldiers also showed a higher volunteering rate than "others." Even when some of the background variables were controlled (e.g., intelligence, European descent of parents, and High School education), some shrinkage in the contrasts occurred, but the Kibbutz-born group was superior to the other two groups in achievement, as indicated by selection for command position, rates of success in officers school, and "advancement in rank."

The author attempts to explain the findings in terms of the child rearing methods prevalent in the Kibbutz. The influence of the educational system upon the motivational levels of the children, the high level of the nursing and educational staff, the better physical conditions and greater attention paid to the children by the staff, as well as possible group pressures from peers, are all listed as probable reasons for the greater success of the Kibbutz-born soldiers. Also considered is the possibility "that the child rearing practices of the Kibbutz are particularly conducive to the development of highly differentiated modes of perception." These, in turn, have been found to be "positively related to success in military functioning."

Bettelheim, B. *The Children of the Dream*. New York: The MacMillan Company, 1969.

After a seven-week stay in Israel, the author presents what he calls "a very personal, impressionistic report, derived from my study of one Kibbutz mainly, though based on observations at several other Kibbutzim." In addition to his observations, the author interviewed many Kibbutz members, former Kibbutz members, and professional authorities outside the Kibbutz, in Israel. He also reviewed the available literature in the area. The result is a volume of over 360 pages replete with various observations on Kibbutz childrearing, motivations of Kibbutz parents, characteristics of Kibbutz-reared children, the future of the Kibbutz, and the possible application of the childrearing principles to American society.

The first chapter titled "an experiment in nature" provides the general background for Bettelheim's study—the rationale, Kibbutz origins, motivations of the founders and special issues such as the status of women. Second is the chapter on "infancy and early childhood" which deals with a description of events and relationships during the first few years of life; weaning, early peer interaction, and the functions and interaction with parents and other adults, as well as the emotional impact of these experiences upon the developing personality, are considered. A discussion of the evolving "collective superego", and the problem of intimacy, conclude this chapter. The third chapter concerns "the latency period" which is viewed by the author as the happiest time in the life of the Sabra. Here dynamic issues, especially "oedipal relations" and the problem of multiple mothering and its effects are dealt with extensively. Adolescence, which, on the other hand, is seen as a period full of tension and unhappiness because of the restrictions on the Sabra's freedom in a number of areas, is the topic of chapter four. Chapters 5 and 6 contain discussions of the "results of Kibbutz education" and an analysis of the Kibbutz personality in terms of Erickson's developmental stages. Although some of the author's conclusions are rather controversial, he points out many interesting problems which are worthy of systematic investigation. Several brief appendixes, which conclude the book, present very sketchily a description of the methods of investigation employed by the author and of the setting—a Kibbutz named "Atid" (fictitious)—where he sojourned.

Caplan, G. Clinical observations on the emotional life of children in the communal settlements of Israel. In *Problems of Infancy and Childhood: Transactions of the Seventh Conference.* **Edited by M.S.E. Senn. New York: Josiah Macy, Jr. Foundation, 1954.**

A descriptive account of collective education prefaced by a brief historical survey of the motives for the establishment and development of the system of Kibbutz childrearing. The main findings reported, based on relatively brief visits to a number of Kibbutzim, are as follows: children 5–7 years of age and below manifest emotional disturbance implied by such symptoms as thumbsucking, temper tantrums, and lack of control of aggression. Enuresis is also a major problem and the young "Kibbutz children look as though they are suffering from maternal deprivation." Later, the children have fewer problems, "have a much smoother adolescence," and grow up to be "remarkably non-neurotic" young adults.

A stimulating interchange between conferees who participated at the meeting where the paper was presented accompanies the article. A number of questions related to the observations reported by Caplan were raised by the participants.

1. To what extent is there a reduction of individual differences among Kibbutz children due to the uniformity in the childrearing practices?
2. Is the Kibbutz-reared adult an emotionally mature person?
3. Were the relatively favorably-viewed adolescents similar in their earlier years to the younger "maladjusted" children described in the report?

Eisenberg, L., and Neubauer, P.B. Mental health issues in Israeli collectives: Kibbutzim. *Journal of the American Academy of Child Psychiatry,* **1965, 4: 426–442.**

"Qualitative reflections," based on a six-day colloquium with Israeli colleagues and upon visits to several Kibbutzim, describe the authors' observations in this article. There is also some reference to previously published research. Several topics are of major concern to the authors. With respect to *Parent-Child relations* they see the Kibbutz setting as a *col-*

laborative child rearing program rather than an abdication of the childrearing functions by the parents. The importance is in the congruence between the parents' and educators' objectives. "There can be more than one child-rearing person as long as the child can unify them into a single image." When there was dissonance between parents and educators then problems occurred in the children. As to *adolescence and identity formation* and the relative absence of rebellion in Kibbutz adolescents, they view the major reasons as due to the mobilization of aggression against the external enemies and the great challenge of inhospitable physical surroundings. These "syntonic targets" absorb energy. There is a fulfillment of the pioneering ideals on the part of the second generation. *The absence of homosexuality* is considered next. Since the psychopathology of the family has been viewed as the major cause of homosexuality, "The Kibbutz child has the potential mitigating influences of the coeducators and therefore has the opportunity for a corrective experience against these parental influences." They also quote Nagler regarding the possibility for "diluting pathological oedipal conflicts." Finally, the discussion centers upon Kibbutz attitudes toward higher education which is viewed as inconsistent with Kibbutz needs and ideology. Also, the article includes a brief description of the "purification" ritual or group self-evaluation among adolescents and its potency in strengthening Kibbutz ties.

Handel, A. Self-concept of the Kibbutz adolescent (Hebrew), *Megamot,* **1961, 11, 142–159.**

A "modified Q-sort" technique was employed in this study of 81 city and 70 Kibbutz twelfth graders. A number of significant differences in self-rating between the two groups were obtained. Kibbutz adolescents view themselves as less self-confident in facing difficulties, trust their future less, more often deride themselves and feel helpless. They are also less optimistic than city adolescents, view themselves as somewhat less intelligent and more sensitive to criticism. They also manifest great anxiety in critical situations and in facing strangers. On the other hand, Kibbutz adolescents are less indifferent to the environment, other people's troubles touch them more readily, and they are more ready to act in consonance with their conscience. More than the city adolescent, his Kibbutz counterpart is ready to act in opposition to parents and custom, but is more tied to his home and misses it even after leaving for a short time; he is sociable, social isolation is harder for him to bear, and he finds it more difficult to be separated from a beloved person. In terms of needs, "blaimavoidance" and "infravoidance" are greater in Kibbutz youngsters. Overall, the "index of adjustment" favors the city adolescents.

Hes, J. P., and Levine, J. Kibbutz humor. *The Journal of Nervous and Mental Diseases*, 1962, 155: 327–331.

By studying content of humor, which is considered a means of relief from anxiety and tension, the authors propose to uncover the areas of problems and covert conflicts of Kibbutzniks. Popular cartoons published by two members of different Kibbutzim were classified into three subcategories of problems related to the search for equality: "1) the problem of power and authority; 2) the theme of sharing social responsibility; and 3) the attitude of the Kibbutznik towards art and culture." Cartoons about the first theme show the child as the authority. Adults appear as helpless slaves to the demanding children who have little respect for them.

Cartoons about the second category show a derisive attitude toward management which is seen as inept and impotent; there is an unwillingness to undertake responsibilities. Management is insensitive to individual needs. "In essence, attitudes about management really reflect the ambivalences Kibbutzniks feel toward the Kibbutz itself." Art and culture in conflict with work appear to be reflected in the third set of cartoons; with work apparently gaining the upper hand. In concluding the paper, the authors raise the question of the future viability of the Kibbutz, the possibility that its mission has been accomplished and that the spartan rigors of pioneering may no longer be necessary.

Irvine, Elizabeth E. Children in Kibbutzim: thirteen years after. *Journal of Child Psychology and Psychiatry,* **1966, 7: 167–178.**

A review of some of the highlights of a 1963 seminar held in Israel in which American and Israeli educators and mental health workers discussed collective education (reported in the volume edited by Neubauer). Some of the recent comparative research on personality development in Kibbutz and non-Kibbutz children was also reviewed.

Irvine, Elizabeth. Observations of the aims and methods of child rearing in communal settlements in Israel. *Human Relations,* **1952, 5: 247–275.**

One of the first psychologically-oriented presentations of Kibbutz child-rearing by a Western observer, primarily from the psychodynamic viewpoint. Some of the observation and comments are "dated" for they apply to Kibbutz practices of that period (circa 1950). Toilet-training, coeducation, and sexuality are examples. The author, however, tries to come to grips with some basic psychodynamic issues which are central to "collective education"; deprivation and divided loyalties of the child" vis á vis different parental figures, identification and super ego formation, etc. are some of the areas about which observations are made and speculations offered. Some of the observations have been disputed and questions are raised regarding their representativeness (e.g., "Young children . . . appear apathetic compared with children in more stimulating environments"). The interpretations offered (e.g., "The listlessness or apathy of the children seemed to be related to a lack of security etc.") have also been questioned. Yet, many of these speculations have served as a stimulus for further systematic research and observation that followed.

Kaffman, M. Evaluation of emotional disturbance in 403 Israeli Kibbutz children. *American Journal of Psychiatry,* **1962, 97: 732-738.**

A survey of the frequency and intensity of behavior problems in a sample of 403 children, aged 1–12 years from three different Kibbutzim reveals that the "findings seem either to match the usual figures in 'normal controls' or even appeared less prominently." Aggression, temper tantrums, breath holding attacks, enuresis, rhythmic motor habits, speech problems, nail biting, and night fears were the symptoms surveyed. "A very peculiar difference is the inverted ratio between thumbsucking and eating problems," with the Kibbutz children showing three times more thumbsucking and only a third as many eating problems as in the controls. The greater frequency of thumbsucking is explained on the basis of early weaning and greater permissiveness in the attitude of adults to the habit. Low frequency of eating problems is considered to be due to the fact that the nurse (metapelet) rather than the biological mother is in charge of training the infants. The author concludes with the opinion that, in the majority of cases, deviation in Kibbutz children is due "to a disturbed child-parent relationship.'

Kaffman, M. A comparison of Psychopathology: Israeli children from Kibbutz and from urban surroundings. *American Journal of Orthopsychiatry,* **1965, 35: 509–520.**

Two groups of emotionally disturbed children, eighty-four from Kibbutzim and ninety-seven non-Kibbutz urban area children (Hollingshead's classes III, IV, and V), who were referred to clinics were compared with respect to the incidence of psychiatric diagnosis. All children were diagnosed by the same psychiatrist (author) who served as psychiatric consultant to the city and Kibbutz clinics. The bulk of both groups placed within three major diagnostic categories: "Primary behavior problems," "neurotic traits," and "psychoneurotic disorders" (about 80 per cent). Small numbers were also diagnosed as psychotic, "personality trait disturbance," etc.

Essentially, there were no significant differences in the incidence of the several disorders between the groups. The only marked difference occurs in the diagnosis of "sociopathic personality"; seven urban children were placed in this category and none from the Kibbutzim. Also, there were more disturbed preschool children in the urban group, preschool problems being handled for the most part locally in each Kibbutz.

A unique clinical syndrome, the "outcast child" is found in the Kibbutz group (six cases, aged 8–12). In these cases, "a mutual antagonistic relationship between the child and

76

his group is found with a circular reaction of self and group exclusion." These children are isolates and are "overwhelmed by total group rejection." "They do not conform to school and group requirements and wander around the Kibbutz alone" truanting without any clear purpose. The primary causal factor of the "outcast child" is seen in a "severely disturbed parent-child relationship."

Methodologically, some of the major problems with this study are the low socioeconomic status of the control (non-Kibbutz) sample and the possible sources of error in making the diagnostic decisions.

Kaffman, M. Survey of opinions and attitudes of Kibbutz members toward mental illness: preliminary report. *The Israel Annals of Psychiatry and Related Disciplines,* **1967, 5: 17–31.**

Preliminary results of a survey, concerning attitudes toward mental health and treatment, of 200 Kibbutz members are reported in this paper. Of 200 Kibbutz members questioned, 86% expressed readiness to work with a person who had been hospitalized for mental reasons; however, only 39% "would consent to the marriage of that patient to a relative." In case of behavior disturbance of the child of a friend, 68% would recommend psychiatric or psychological treatment. Not so in case of adults: only 38% would recommend the use of clinics or other assistance. Other professionals were recommended. Nonprofessional suggestions in the case of prolonged depression were proposed by 46% of the respondents. Of these, 25% suggested that one should "try to overcome yourself." Eight percent suggested that a depressed person should "consult with an experienced friend." Such nonprofessional counselors who inspire confidence are apparently to be found in every Kibbutz. Only three out of the 200 respondents would recommend suspension of work in case of a depressed person. Many stress the therapeutic value of work and maintenance of contact with reality. These data are discussed in light of available comparable data in other cultures. The author's general impression is that "there exists an inclination toward greater tolerance of the mentally ill, willingness to help him recover . . ." in Kibbutz society as compared with the attitudes twenty years previously.

Kardiner, A. The roads to suspicion, rage, apathy, and societal disintegration. In I. Galdson (ed.), *Beyond the Germ Theory*. New York: Health Education Council, 1954.

This article is chiefly concerned with the relationship between "social emotions" and social structure. According to the author "it seems evident that the monogamous, patriarchally oriented family has proved the most successful, the most plastic, and the most viable." The Kibbutz is one of the illustrations of contrast considered in this context. Child-rearing in the Kibbutz is described as a process in which "Routine and simultaneity are emphasized. Children move their bowels together, eat together, and so forth. There is little opportunity for affective exchange except with their contemporaries." The outcome is that the "human unit is egocentric and envious, with little capacity for affective relationship, a good deal of mistrust, and a good deal of mutual contempt." Also, the author feels that "the social emotions are learned but not integrated" by Kibbutz children. In addition, Kardiner further concludes that Kibbutz members are well-controlled and do not allow "a breakdown of the learned social behavior to the extent that the society is abandoned to uncontrolled anxiety and rage." There is a repression of envy and greed, high self criticism, and social vigilance. The society as a whole is viewed as the individual's source of security, rather than interpersonal relationships.

Kugelmass, S. and Breznitz, S. Perception of parents by Kibbutz adolescents: A further test of the instrumentality-expressivity model. *Human Relations,* **1966, 19 (1): 117–122.**

Using a model of perceptual behavior, based on "instrumentality-expressivity," a group of Kibbutz adolescents were asked to evaluate their parents. Results indicate that the same-sex parent was seen as more "instrumental," while the opposite-sex parent was viewed as more "expressive."

Kugelmass, S., and Breznitz, S. The development of intentionality in moral judgment in city and Kibbutz adolescents. *The Journal of Genetic Psychology,* **1967, 111: 103–111.**

Piaget's theory of moral judgment regarding the transition from use of results (objective responsibility) to intentionality (subjective responsibility) serves as the starting point for this study of 1014 city children and 456 Kibbutz children, eleven to seventeen years of age. Since "Piaget considered the influence of parental authority as an inhibiting factor, and the developing peer group as a positively stimulating influence in the progressive transition from objective to subjective responsibility," it was expected that differences in socialization between city and Kibbutz children will show different developmental tendencies in this process. A questionnaire designed to test extent of use of intentionality and awareness of the principles involved did not yield significant differences between the city and Kibbutz children. It is concluded that "this type of *cognitive* development is strongly age-related through adolescence.

Luria, Zella, Goldwasser, M., and Goldwasser, A.
Response to transgression in stories by Israeli Children.
Child Development, **1963, 34: 271–280.**

Responses to four incomplete stories (transgression against mother's command, death wish against an adult coach, breaking of a minor pledge to a peer group, and cheating in a sport contest) by forty-six Kibbutz and twenty-six Moshav children, aged 11–13 years, were compared. These were also compared with data on thirty-seven Jewish American and on 101 Gentile American children.

The results indicate that Kibbutz children confess more readily than Moshav children. The Israeli as well as the American Jewish children do not show the sex differences reported in the Gentile American children. In the latter group the number of confessions of girls is significantly higher than among the boys. Jewish girls confess less than Gentile girls, accounting for the lack of sex differences in the Jewish groups. The Kibbutz mother's weapon of "giving love" is seen as a major factor in inducing confessions.

Nagler, S. Clinical observations on Kibbutz children. *The Israeli Annals of Psychiatry and Related Disciplines,* **1963, 1: 201–216.**

Intimate knowledge of the problems of Kibbutz children and their parents is reflected in this article by a longtime consultant and psychotherapist working in the Kibbutz movement. In general, he finds that the frequency of occurrence of disturbance among Kibbutz children is about the same as in the general population; "all the usual symptoms, syndromes and clinical categories occur." There seems to be a greater incidence of thumbsucking and less frequent eating problems among Kibbutz children. Also, juvenile delinquency and male homosexuality are extremely rare.

From the viewpoint of dynamics the author sees the parent-child relationship as more decisive in the pathogenic process than the educational structure itself. He particularly stresses the pathogenic influence of disturbed interaction and relationships between parents and educators (metapelet, teachers etc.). Additional points of stress were: parents' conflicts over collective education, unchangeability of environment and fixed social status of child, excessive organization of adolescent's activities, lack of professional training opportunities, etc. Some of the "pluses" considered are: opportunities for corrective emotional experiences in the group, possibility of diluting Oedipal conflicts via transference to educators and to the other children, etc. This valuable paper offers a wealth of first-hand observations, and theoretical generalizations and insights which few persons besides the author are in a position to make.

Neubauer, P. B. *Children in Collectives* (child-rearing aims and practices in the Kibbutz). Springfield, Ill.: Charles C. Thomas, 1965.

A group of Western (mostly American) psychiatrists and educators visited a number of Kibbutzim and held a joint conference with a group of Kibbutz educators and other leaders of Israeli education. In this volume the details of the impressions of the visitors and the exchange of ideas between them and the Kibbutz educators are reported. In addition to a presentation of the "fundamental concepts" of Kibbutz education and a discussion of these concepts, reports of the visitors to the Kibbutzim and a discussion of these reports are included. The rest of the book is devoted to presentations (by Kibbutz educators) and discussions (by Israelis and Americans) of "early childhood and latency," "adolescence," and "family life and the role of women." In the final section, prior to the "concluding remarks," there is a report on a "special session" which includes brief reports on a miscellany of topics—about children in the USA, Holland, and Great Britain—as well as two articles on psychopathology among Kibbutz children.

Pelled, N. On the formation of object-relations and identifications of the Kibbutz child. *The Israel Annals of Psychiatry and Allied Disciplines, 1964,* **2**: 144–161.

It is the main contention of the author that the mother serves as the "main object-relation" for the Kibbutz child. Metaplot, educators, and other closely related adults are seen as objects in need-satisfying and "transient-interchangeable" relationships.

A number of case studies are marshalled in support of this thesis. It is also felt that the parents are the main identification objects. Moreover, the author observes that "In cases known to me, I could not observe any dilution or relief of the Oedipal conflicts. Often the contrary occurred; the children felt that they were evicted not only from the intimacy of their parents—i.e., the parents' bedroom—but also from their own home." Furthermore, it also appears that "the conflicts connected with sexual curiosity about the parents, with sex-identification, and with experience with the primal scene, real or phantasied, are no different from those which can be observed in children living with their families. Much of the psychoanalytically-oriented theoretical discussion concerns also the fusion of the metapelet into the gestalt of the mother. The conclusions are drawn from the author's long-time experience as a psychotherapist with emotionally disturbed Kibbutz-born children and adults.

Preale, Ilana, Amir, Y., and Sharan (Singer) S., Perceptual articulation and task effectiveness in several Israel sub-cultures. *Journal of Personality and Social Psychology* **1970, 15(3): 190–195. (Also in** *Megamot* **(Hebrew), 1970).**

Employing Witkin's theoretical framework, the authors arrive at one prediction that "Kibbutz subjects will achieve higher scores on tests of perceptual articulation than will non-Kibbutz subjects." The main reasons for this expectation was the stress upon autonomy in Kibbutz child-rearing and the anticipated "positive relationships between measures of perceptual articulation and achievement on complex social tasks." (Available data on the success of Kibbutz-born young men in positions of military leadership support the second reason.)

As part of this larger study, also involving comparisons on the basis of ethnic background, 145 Kibbutz young men were compared with the same number of non-Kibbutz subjects on the Embedded Figures Test, on Block Design (Wechsler), and on the Figure drawing. Actually, only 60 S's were compared on all three tests; all S's took the Embedded Figures Test. All subjects were being tested as officer candidates for the Israel Defense Force, and the groups were matched for level of intelligence since a positive correlation between perceptual articulation and IQ was reported.

The obtained results confirm the prediction in part. Kibbutz subjects performed remarkably better than the non-Kibbutz subjects on the Embedded Figures Test and on the Figure Drawing (p = .02). There were no statistically significant differences on the Block Design Test.

Rabin, A. I. Personality maturity of Kibbutz (Israeli collective settlement) and non-Kibbutz children as reflected in Rorschach. *Journal of Projective Techniques,* **1957, 21: 148–153.**

In order to test the effects of absence of "continuous mothering" in infancy upon later personality development in childhood, thirty-eight Kibbutz reared ten-year olds and thirty-four controls were compared by means of the Rorschach technique. Formal scores and ratios, along with global evaluations of personality maturity made by three judges on the basis of the scoring summaries, constituted the dimensions for comparison. Significant differences between the groups with respect to Dd and F plus percentages in a direction favoring greater maturity of the Kibbutz group were obtained. Differences with respect to C, CF and FC relationships, number of content categories and overall personality maturity ratings approach significance. No differences in the incidence of P, H, and A% or in the Experience Balance were obtained. The following conclusions may be drawn:

1. Kibbutz children do not reflect, in their formal Rorschach findings, any deleterious effects due to the alleged early maternal "deprivation."

2. There is some evidence that the Kibbutz children show greater personality maturity than do the controls.

3. These results do not support the notion of greater uniformity in the personalities of children reared together under the Kibbutz conditions.

4. Differences between the Kibbutz and the typical institution may account for the dissimilarity in personality development of children under the two sets of conditions.

Rabin, A. I. The Israeli Kibbutz (collective settlement) as a "laboratory" for testing psychodynamic hypotheses. *The Psychological Record.* **1957, 7: 111–115.**

Following a discussion of the use of different social settings for naturalistic experiments and based on a statement concerning the main features of Kibbutz childrearing, the author suggests testing several psychodynamic hypotheses in the Kibbutz "laboratory." On the basis of the maternal deprivation hypothesis and of psychoanalytic theory, the following predictions were made regarding Kibbutz children (as compared with children reared in the ordinary family setting):-

A. Retardation of infants
B. Greater impulsivity and greater emotional and intellectual immaturity
C. Less evidence of strong attachment to parent of the opposite sex
D. Less consistent identification with the parent of the same sex
E. Freer expression of hostility toward parents
F. Less sibling rivalry.

Rabin, A. I. Kibbutz children—research finding to date. *Children*, **1958, 5: 179–184.**

This article contains a brief description of Kibbutz child-rearing procedures and an outline of a research program. Preliminary findings, elaborated upon in subsequent publications by the author, are presented in non-technical language. Brief reports of developmental data on infants and personality study of ten-year-olds are included. The children's attitude toward their biological parents as well as interaction with the interviewer-researcher are also reported and described.

Rabin, A. I. Some psychosexual differences between Kibbutz and non-Kibbutz Israeli boys. *Journal of Projective Techniques*, **1958, 22: 328–332.**
Also in: *Theory and Research in Abnormal Psychology.* **Edited by Rosenhan & London. New York: Holt, Rinehart and Winston, 1969.**

A group of 27 ten-year old boys from patriarchal-type families were compared with a group of 27 boys who were reared in the Kibbutz (collective settlement) with respect to three psychosexual dimensions: Oedipal intensity, positive identification, and sibling rivalry. The structured response items of the Blacky Test inquiry were used as a basis for comparison. Consistent with the stated hypotheses, the experimental group gave evidence of lesser Oedipal intensity, more diffuse positive identification, and less intense sibling rivalry.

Rabin, A. I. Attitudes of Kibbutz children to family and parents. *The American Journal of Orthopsychiatry*, 1959, 29: 172–179.

Sentence completion results of ninety-two Kibbutz-reared and forty-five control children, between the ages of nine and eleven, were compared with respect to their attitudes in three areas of intrafamilial relationships—family, father and mother. The results are based on individual item analyses and on ratings of area clusters by three judges. The trends obtained are as follows:

1. More Kibbutz children show clearly positive attitudes toward the family than do non-Kibbutz children.

2. Control girls more frequently show positive attitudes toward the father than do Kibbutz girls. No differences between the boys, in this respect, were obtained.

3. More Kibbutz boys show positive attitudes toward the mother than do non-Kibbutz boys. No differences between the girls were obtained.

The theoretical implications of the findings were discussed in terms of ambivalence related to socialization during the child-rearing process. Some of the inconsistencies of the results may serve as guideposts for further research.

Rabin, A. I. Kibbutz adolescents. *The American Journal of Orthopsychiatry*, 1961, 31: 493–504.
In Rosenblith and Allinsmith (eds.). *The Causes of Behavior II*. Boston: Allyn & Bacon, 1966. Also in D. Rogers (ed.). *Issues in Adolescent Psychology*. New York: Appleton-Century-Crofts, 1969. Also in I. Al-Issa and Dennis, W. (eds.), *Cross-Cultural Studies of Behavior*. New York: Holt, Rinehart & Winston, 1970.

In an attempt to tease out some of the psychological differences between Kibbutz-reared adolescents and adolescents (controls) reared in the conventional family and social setting, three projective techniques (Rorschach, Sentence Completion and TAT) were administered to two parallel groups of 17-year-olds. From the data presented, it was concluded that the Kibbutz adolescent is at least as well adjusted as his non-Kibbutz counterpart; there is some evidence that he is more spontaneous and at least as intelligent. The Kibbutz adolescent does not seem to differ from the control with respect to positiveness of attitude to parents; also, he tends to be less in conflict with them and to involve them less in his fantasy production. He is more rigidly concerned with taboos on premarital sexuality, less self-motivated and less 'ambitious' in our conventional sense.

The results were discussed and related to differences in life experience, stemming from differences in the social structure, to which the two groups have been exposed.

Rabin, A. I. **Personality study in Israeli Kibbutzim.** In B. Kaplan (ed.). *Studying Personality Cross-Culturally.* Evanston, Illinois: Row and Peterson, 1961.

As one of the "case studies" in cross-cultural research in this volume, the discussion focuses on the problems of doing field work in a highly literate Western-type of society, in the Israeli Kibbutz. This chapter stresses the differences between the anthropologist and psychologist concerned with the cross-cultural study of personality variables and with testing psychodynamic hypotheses. Special attention is paid to the nature of the Kibbutz subculture, its leadership, and the rank and file in their relations and attitudes to the outside observers and social science investigators. Some unique characteristics of the interaction between the researcher and Kibbutz adults and children are also considered.

Rabin, A. I. *Growing up in the Kibbutz*. New York: Springer Publishing Company, 1965. Japanese Translation (Z. Kusakari, tr.) Tokyo: Taisei Shuppan Ltd., 1970.

Following a descriptive chapter concerning Kibbutz child-rearing and education, the author poses a number of questions revolving around personality development of the Kibbutz child. Kibbutz infants, preadolescents, and adolescents of both sexes are compared with parallel Moshav groups of children on a number of personality variables elicited by means of structured and projective techniques. A small sample of Kibbutz-reared soldiers is also compared with a group of non-Kibbutz-reared soldiers by means of data obtained from the files of the Israeli Defense Forces training and classification unit.

The findings indicate that the exposure of Kibbutz children to "partial maternal deprivation" does not handicap them nor interfere with healthy personality development. It is concluded that multiple mothering has no deleterious effects on the evolving personality. Despite some early slow-down in developmental tempo, Kibbutz children catch up and even surpass their non-Kibbutz counterpart. The "dispersal of cathexis" in relation to other adults, in addition to the parents, is seen as beneficial to many children. Moreover, the lower intensity in the identification process and the utilization of adults as well as peer models appears to be adequate in developing moral attitudes and adequate sex-appropriate roles. The book concludes by pointing out the opportunities for closer affiliation and security and less feeling of alienation among Kibbutz-reared youngsters as compared with those in our own society.

Rabin, A. I. and Goldman, Hanna. The relationship of severity of guilt to intensity of identification in Kibbutz and non-Kibbutz children. *The Journal of Social Psychology*, 1966, 69: 159–163.

The prediction that Kibbutz children, because of more diffuse and less intense identification, show less severity of guilt upon violation of social norms than non-Kibbutz children was made. Two different series of four incomplete stories that deal with the violation of social norms (theft, disobedience, death wishes, and sabotage of group effort) were administered to groups of Kibbutz and non-Kibbutz boys and girls respectively. The results indicate support for the hypothesis.

These results are based on a comparison of the responses of fifty-four boys and fifty-six girls born in the Kibbutz with fifty-two boys and forty-eight girls reared in conventional family settings (controls). The median age for all groups was thirteen years. All were seventh graders.

Shapira, A., and Madsen, M. C. Cooperative and competitive behavior of Kibbutz and urban children in Israel. *Child Development*, 1969, 40: 609–618.

Forty Kibbutz-reared children, and forty urban children from an upper middle-class community, ages 6–10, were studied with the Madsen Cooperation Board. The two experiments performed were designed to compare the degree of cooperative and competitive behavior in the two groups. Under conditions of group reward, both groups cooperated adaptively. However, when conditions were changed from group to individual reward, the urban children began to compete "in a nonadaptive manner," while the Kibbutz children persisted in their cooperative behavior. Kibbutz children also tended to be less competitive than the urban children even in the second experiment "in which competitive responding was more adaptive than in the first." The results are viewed as confirming the hypothesis that Kibbutz children would show more cooperative behavior than city children.

Spiro, M. E. *Children of the Kibbutz*. Cambridge, Mass: Harvard University Press, 1958.

This nearly 500 page volume represents the most comprehensive statement describing "collective education" that is available. It represents the detailed and painstaking observations that the author, an anthropologist, and his wife have made over a year's stay as participant observers in the Kibbutz (Kiryat Yedidim—fictitious name). It is a "second volume" and an extension of "Kibbutz: Venture in Utopia" which was published two years earlier and presented a more general account of various aspects of Kibbutz structure and life.

The book is divided into six parts. Part I gives an introductory overview of Kibbutz education; Part II deals with "agents of socialization"—the metapelet, nursery teacher, parents and other adults; Part III is entirely devoted to the "first year" of life; Part IV, entitled "the tender age," focuses on a number of theoretical issues, the socialization of different behavior systems, and ends with a chapter on the "Oedipus complex and sexual identity." In the next Part V ("school years")—primary and secondary school, formal educational activities, work experience, social interaction and activities, and issues relating to sex—are treated in some detail. Finally, chapter VI involves a critical analysis of the personality of the Kibbutz childrearing product—the "Sabras." Here, the transition of the adolescent to adult status is considered, as are his assumptions of the roles of husband and father. Furthermore, discussion of conformity and superego development in view of the different childrearing conditions and similarity of environment are considered in some detail. Finally, the constellation of several salient personality traits that characterize the Sabras are presented with supporting episodic material and observation. These traits are introversion, hostility, insecurity and inferiority feelings. There are three appendixes: one discusses briefly the methods employed in the investigation (observation, interviews, questionnaire, documents and publications, and projective tests), the second reports the high school curriculum, and the third presents some numerical data on the "Stewart Emotional Response Test" and on a moral ideology test (Bavelas).

IX   CHILD DEVELOPMENT AND EDUCATION

Bar-Yoseph, R. Patterns of early socialization in the collective settlements in Israel. *Human Relations*, 1959, 12: 345–360.

The paper is an attempt to compare the framework of socialization of the young child in the Kibbutzim in Israel with the social pattern that frames the life of the adults. Adult life is centered around group membership and social responsibility.

The child grows up with two separate "homes." One is the nursery and the other is the parents' home. By traversing daily from one to the other they get an idea of the settlement as a whole which becomes known as "ours." As everything is geared according to the work schedule, including at first feeding schedules of infants and later visits by the parents and finally visits to the parents' home, the children quickly develop the concept of "work." Because of the children's diverse interactions with many nurses, their parents' neighbors, their peers' parents, their siblings, and their peers, as well as the other friendly adults, the children develop a sense of the Kibbutz member. They develop the sense of being part of a community.

An important aspect in developing a sense of group membership is their having to share the attention of the nurse. She is not readily available, so the children learn to identify with her and satisfy each other's needs by taking turns at playing nurse and playing child. The nurse encourages this, and thereby reduces frustration. As identifications with the nurse extend to the peer group, relationships with peers are not heavily loaded emotionally and emphasize performance, doing things together or for each other. The children are free to express aggression in the peer group. The group is relatively unstructured and the nurse allows a great deal of free play. As a result of the testing of aggressive and assertive acts in the free play situation, the child learns some of the basic principles of interpersonal relationship with equals.

Bettelheim, B. Does communal education work? *Commentary*, **1962, 34: 117–125.**

It has been shown that children brought up communally are relatively free of asocial behaviors and in addition the Kibbutzim are "exceedingly effective in rearing their children to live up to the basic moral principles which they share with the larger society." The author defends the idea of the continuity and consistency of the Kibbutz mother-child relationship and the continuity and consistency of the child with his enviroment.

The child does have a continuous relationship with his parents whom he sees every day. What's more, the Kibbutz child has the security of a continuous relationship with his peers. In contrast to the American child, who has to endure his anxieties alone in his room, the Kibbutz children share intimate experiences and know exactly what each is afraid of and therefore reassure each other. The anxious child knows he can trust his comrades and feels absolutely secure when he is with the other children. In the Kibbutz setup the children also are much more involved in their parents' community than American children are. They are made to feel accepted as active participants of the community, something quite lacking in American society.

The Kibbutz educational system is judged on the basis of how well it attains its goals. The specific goals or values that Kibbutzim set out to instill—in order of importance—are "work," "love of humanity," "responsibility to the Kibbutz," etc. According to the author these goals are achieved without parallel anywhere else.

The non-competitive school system produces students superior to our own. The main motive of forming the educational system to make the child independent of his parents is also realized. The intensity of feeling is lacking towards parents, but is rather concentrated on the peers with whom one was brought up. While the parental intensity is lacking, so is all the guilt and conflict over dependency strivings and projected parental fears and guilts. Instead of adopting the idiosyncracies of one or two parents, multiple mothering prevents too strong identifications with one person. Rather, the children adopt the consistent patterns and values of the community.

Faigin, Helen. **Social behavior of young children in the Kibbutz.** *Journal of Abnormal and Social Psychology.* **1958, 46, 117–129.**

In addition to a discussion of the functions of the metapelet as a socializing agent, as a housekeeper, caretaker, and educator, this article is concerned with the question whether toddlers can learn social interaction and group identification in a setting of group-living. Three groups of toddlers were observed systematically in each of two Kibbutzim. Statistical data of the observations on aggression and dependency are reported. The children, between the ages of nineteen and thirty-eight months, develop a strong group identification (frequent use of "we," "ours," and "theirs") and defend members of their own group from attack by members of another group. Competition is ordinarily between groups rather than within groups. Children in the group tend to exercise control of each other's behavior. There are some differences between the behavior of children in one Kibbutz where childrearing is more structured and controlled as compared with the other where it is more casual. The youngest children in the former showed more dependency responses whereas in the latter there is more frequent thumbsucking and crying. Also, the children in the first Kibbutz developed faster (greater awareness of surroundings, spoke earlier) than the children in the second Kibbutz. No such differences were noted in the older groups.

Gewirtz, Hava B., and Gewirtz, J.L. Caretaking settings, background events and behavior differences in four Israeli child-rearing environments: some preliminary trends. In B.M. Foss (ed.), *Determinants of infant behaviour, IV.* London: Methuen Co. Ltd., 1969.

In addition to general methodological aims, the purpose of the report is to attempt a description of the specific "stimulus conditions" in the Kibbutz infant's setting and the pattern of the infant's responses as they compare with familial and institutional environments. A group of twenty 26-week-old infants, from four different environments (institution, Kibbutz, youngest child in family, and single-child), five from each setting, were closely observed. Considering the percentage of time subjects are awake, the institutional setting seems to "provide the least variation in terms of total caretaking time, of visits by persons other than caretakers, and of exposure to locations other than the 'home room.' " Kibbutz and multiple-child-family infants seem to be most exposed to such variations. In institutions and single-child families, the caretaker or mother seems to spend more time in the infant's vicinity than is true in the other two settings. Some data regarding the caretakers' behavior and infants' reactions are also reported, preliminary to more sophisticated study of "interaction sequences." "Median smile and vocal rates of institutional infants appear about half or less of what they are for infants in the other environments; . . . institution infants

96

. . . appear to be exposed to the lowest rate of adult talking and smiling. Mothers of single-child-family infants seem to exhibit the highest overall rate of talking towards their infants, and *Kibbutz* mothers seem to smile more to their infants than do mothers of urban families." The tables report "descriptive statistical data" in terms of means, medians, and ranges of "talk," "smile," "vocalize," etc. Thus, the reported characteristics and differences are mainly trends, rather than final results.

Gewirtz, Hava B., and Gewirtz, J. L. Visiting and caretaking patterns for Kibbutz infants: age and sex trends. *American Journal of Orthopsychiatry,* **1968, 38: 427–443**

Twenty-four Kibbutz infants, twelve at four months of age, and twelve eight-month-olds (16 boys and 8 girls) were observed "in two sessions, morning and afternoon on successive days." The infants were individually observed by a trained observer, and the time spent on sleep, feeding, eating, diaper-changing, dressing, bathing, and medicating was recorded. Also, the amount of contact with mother, caretaker (metapelet) and father was noted. The individual logs were summarized and comparisons of age groups and across sexes were made. Although the major purpose of this preliminary report was to illustrate a method, some substantive findings are also reported. It seems that during the first eight months of the Kibbutz infant's life he "sees his mother for at least twice as much time as he sees his father or the main caretaker." During the mornings, mothers were three times as long with younger infants than they were with older ones. Caretaking activities took longer for boys than girls at both age levels. Fathers spent more time with older infants than with younger ones, and with boys more than with girls. The investigators feel that the sex difference patterns tend to indicate that infant boys are initally less "mature" than girls. Time spent on sleep etc., is reported but is probably not unique.

Comparison of these Kibbutz data with similar information on family-reared and institutional infants are expected to follow this interim report.

Gewirtz, J.L. The course of infant smiling in four child-rearing environments in Israel. In B.M. Foss (ed.), *Determinants of infant behavior, III*. New York: John Wiley and Sons, 1965.

Infants from four environments (residential institution, day nursery, town family, and Kibbutz) were exposed for two minutes to the unsmiling face of an observer. There were 226 institutional infants, 105 from nursery, 91 family infants and 236 from different Kibbutzim. With the exception of the day nursery where the infants' ages ranged from 8–18 months, all the other infants' ages were distributed between one and eighteen months. Age curves for "Mean frequency of smiles in 2 minutes" and "Proportion of S's exhibiting some smiles" were constructed for all groups. The conclusion of this initial report is that two smile age patterns have been discerned: "an Institution and Day Nursery pattern, relatively lower in initial and final level; and a family and Kibbutz pattern, relatively higher in initial and final level." Although Kibbutz, family and institution mean age curves are parallel in the first four months, the fist two settings listed do not differ from each other, while both are reliably higher than the institution curve. "The Mean Smile age curve peak is reached at 20 weeks by Institution S's, and at 16 weeks by Kibbutz and Town Family S's." Also, there is a little decline in Kibbutz age curve after the four-months peak, but no

98

decline in the family. After the 4–5 month peak there is a decline in the institution and nursery mean smile and proportion curves. Around eight months, the mean frequency level is similar for all groups; subsequent to that age a decline occurs in all groups. However, a comparison shows that "the family curve showed reliably *less* linear decline than did the other three curves, while the Kibbutz curve declined reliably less than the institution curve." The "abrupt decline in smile rate" after the 4–5 months peak, found by other investigators, was not confirmed in this study.

Golan, S. *Collective education*. (Hebrew.) Tel Aviv: Sifriyat Poalim, 1961.

This is the first volume of the posthumously published collected works by the foremost pioneer and ideologue of Kibbutz childrearing and education. The essays, written and published primarily in the 1940's and 50's cover a wide range of topics—from the ideological foundations and principles of collective education to specific issues involved in the educational process (e.g. the place of the metapelet in the childrearing process, educator-parent relationships, mothering, etc.) and the institutional forms within the collective educational system. Special problems such as coeducational sleeping quarters, poor and slow learners, and health education are also treated.

"Ways and foundations" is the title of the first section of the book. In it the broader theoretical issues underlying collective education are considered. Kibbutz education is viewed "not only as an educational theory, but a political, social, and ideological orientation as well, since it forms a link in the undertakings of a revolutionary movement." Included in this section are also detailed descriptions of collective education, its foundations and realization within the broader setting of Kibbutz society. Stress is laid upon the educational structure at different age levels, upon the curriculum, physical work and the values of the "educational group" (Kvutzah). Also considered are the sociological aspects (woman's position, cooperation and partnership, democracy, and ideological collectivism) and pedagogical aspects of collective education.

The second section entitled "factors of education" (child-rearing and upbringing) is particularly concerned with the significant figures in the life of Kibbutz children—the educators—teachers, metaplot, and parents. Special treatment is given to the problems of interaction between the metaplot and the parents of children in their charge. One of the subsections ends with the following comment: "What is most important is that the educator should be aware that without partnership and cooperation between the educators and the parents, our education will be left fundamentally defective and inadequate." The last and most recent article in this section (1960) deals with "motherhood and maternal care." There is a recognition of some of the ambivalences and doubts some parents have regarding collective upbringing and their share in the process. Golan sees the issue of parenthood as dependent upon the matrix of broader relations, satisfactions and dissatisfactions, in the Kibbutz setting in general.

The third, brief section that concerns the problems of some Kibbutz educational institutions (the infant house, the toddler house, nursery school, and kindergarten) is followed by a rather extensive series of essays on "the social structure in the educational system." Here the author stresses the importance of the "children's society" as fundamental to the system. A good deal of space in this section is devoted to the Kvutzah (group of peers) as the educational unit, its effects in the process of character education, the function of its "mechanech" (adult educator-leader), and the planning of its activities. A number of problematic areas concerning the place of the individual in the group are touched upon. Not least is the issue of strong personal friendships and their relationship to the health and cohesiveness of the Kvutzah.

Section four ("problems and solutions") consists of a miscellany of essays ranging from concerns with criticism of certain aspects of collective education to problems of health and the problems of children who are difficult to educate. The author is concerned with the occasional dissatisfactions of adults with the discipline, studies, etc. of Kibbutz children, and admits the frequent discrepancies between the ideal and the real. He also responds to complaints of a mother who would like to have her children with her by encouraging openness in discussion and by recognizing shortcomings in the educational process in some Kibbutzim —often due to some extenuating circumstances and insufficient concern on the part of the bulk of Kibbutz membership.

The remaining two sections are "stations and achievements" and "in the eyes of strangers." In the former, some historical perspective about educational institutions (in Bet Alpha and Mishmar Haemek) of the Kibbutz Artzi is gained. Concluding the volume are reactions to published works on the Kibbutz (by Western investigators) and to methods of research in Kibbutz education and childrearing.

Golan, S. Collective education in the Kibbutz. *American Journal of Orthopsychiatry,* **1958, 28: 549–556.**

Following a brief, chronologically-ordered description of the stages of the process of collective education in the life of the child, there is a discussion of the emotional bonds between child and mother in the Kibbutz setting. Strong emotional ties and trust during the first year of life are stressed; the secondary role of the *metapelet* during this period is also pointed out. However, during "the second year of life the child is mainly in the hands of the *metapelet.*" The author argues that such arrangements do not involve separation or maternal deprivation in the commonly understood sense of the terms and quotes several authors concerning the health of the product of collective education. Some of the problems discussed involve the failure of *metapelot* to consider individual differences among infants and young children and to spend more time with their charges to the relative neglect of household chores. As to emotional disturbance, "the etiological factor was the relationship with the parents; only for a small minority did we find a connection between the disturbance and the special conditions of collective education."

Golan, S. Collective education in the Kibbutz. *Psychiatry,* 1959, 22: 167–177.

In this primarily descriptive and theoretical article the author discusses several aspects of collective education. Following a brief historical and demographic introduction, Golan concerns himself with Kibbutz education and child-rearing as compared with institutional and family-based settings. He then describes the "structure of Kibbutz education" indicating the typical institutional sequence from birth to maturity. Child-parent relationships are treated in detail and some misapprehensions in the published literature are corrected. Finally, the concluding sections deal with "behavior problems and mental health" and with the special therapeutic values of "social education" in the Kibbutz context.

Golan, S., and Lavi, Z. Communal education, in S. Golan (ed.), *Collective education in the Kibbutz*. Merchavia (Israel): Education Department of the Kibbutz Artzi Hashomer Hatzair, 1961.

After a brief introduction concerning the structure of the Kibbutz, the authors present a detailed and systematic description of education and childrearing in the Kibbutz. The structure of education at different levels, the infant house, the toddlers house, the kindergarten, the junior children's community and the secondary school, is presented. Details about the curriculum and the methods of instruction (by "themes") are also included. The remainder of the article deals with the functions of physical work and with the nature and functions of the educational group. There is also a useful appendix tabulating the work hours of children at different ages, the daily programs of the toddlers house, the elementary and secondary schools, a breakdown of weekly lesson periods (secondary school), and a sample schedule of cultural activities for a week.

Kohen-Raz, R. Mental and motor development of Kibbutz, institutionalized, and home-reared infants in Israel. *Child Development*, 1968, 39: 488–504. Also in *Megamot*, 1968, 15: 366–387.

Three groups of Israeli infants, 130 reared in Kibbutzim, 79 from institutions, and 152 from middle-class homes, were examined with the Bayley Mental and Motor tests. Ages ranged from one to twenty-seven months. The Kibbutz and private-home infants performed on the same level. However, both performed significantly higher on the mental scales and the same on the motor scales when compared with the normative U.S. population. Also, compared with the normative population and with the other two Israeli samples, the institutionalized infants "were significantly retarded mentally and motorically." Finally, "eye-hand coordination and walking appeared relatively less variable cross-culturally and intraculturally than capacity to recover hidden objects, language functions, keeping body equilibrium, and fine motor coordination."

Levin, G. *The influence of the school on the stabilization of children's interpersonal relations.* (Hebrew.) Tel-Aviv: Urim, 1967.

One hundred and eighty-six Kibbutz children and 163 city children, ranging in age from nine to eleven years were asked a series of open-ended questions. The first question: "What is the best thing that comes to your mind, that a teacher can do for a child?" The converse (worst thing) was also asked. The same pairs of questions were asked with respect to father, mother, and classmate. Kibbutz children were also asked the questions in relation to the metapelet. Responses were classified and reported, in percentages, in tabular form. Some general conclusions were also drawn from the results.

First, Kibbutz children use the yardstick of the adult world less than city children. City children cling much more strongly to the values of the adults in their world, whereas this is much less true of the Kibbutz children.

Second, both groups show identification with the same sex adult including deep feelings of a positive nature as well as competitiveness and quarrelsomeness. Attitudes to the opposite sex are characterized by dependency and being pampered.

Third, the image of the teacher in the city is less personal, not so close, and less friendly than in the Kibbutz.

Fourth, Kibbutz children expect a more positive feeling relationship with their parents and view them as more permissive than the city children do.

Fifth, city children expect primarily a materialistic partnership with their classmates, while the Kibbutz children see their peers in the group as fuller partners in their emotional life.

Finally, it was noted that corporal punishment is apparently fairly widespread in both settings.

Marcus, J., Thomas, A., and Chess, S. Behavioral individuality in Kibbutz children. *The Israel Annals of Psychiatry and Related Disciplines,* **1969, 7: 43–54.**

As an antidote to the allegedly prevalent trend in the literature to stress the child-environment interaction in the Kibbutz and the similarities between Kibbutz children, the authors present a study which emphasizes the individuality and variability among Kibbutz children. "As we shall try to show in this report, there is no such child as a "Kibbutz child'."

A group of six children (a Kvutzah) served as the subjects of the study. Their metapelet was intensively interviewed when the children were between three and one-half and four years of age, and again one and a half years later. The authors' concern was with observed behavior which was classifiable into the nine temperament categories (activity level, rhythmicity, approach or withdrawal etc.) employed by Alexander Thomas and collaborators in the New York longitudinal projects. The obtained scores indicate considerable temperamental variability among the children. Some illustrative material is presented, but complete quantitative data are not included. The authors feel, on the basis of the behavioral descriptive data, "that *individuality and variability characterize the children's personalities and their responses to similar environmental stimuli."*

Ortar, Gina A. Educational achievement of primary school graduates in Israel as related to their socio-cultural background. *Comparative Education*, 1967, 4: 23–34.

Only one particular finding relating Kibbutz children is reported within the context of this broader study of educational achievement of different groups of primary school pupils in Israel. Based on a 1955 nation-wide survey it was found that, generally, boys were superior to girls on the subjects tested (geography, arithmetic, Bible study, vocabulary, and history). However, sex-differences were lowest for the Kibbutz children as compared with the other groups (cities, villages, and temporary immigrant settlements). Kibbutz boys were also superior to girls on all subjects but the vocabulary test, on which there were no differences in achievement between the sexes.

Rabin, A. I. Children's Apperception Test findings with Kibbutz and non-Kibbutz preschoolers. *Journal of Projective Techniques and Personality Assessment*, 1968, 32: 420–424.

Tables report comparative CAT data on forty-three (nineteen boys and twenty-four girls) Kibbutz and thirty-six (sixteen boys and twenty girls) Moshav preschoolers (ages 5–6 years). Mention of parents in the stories and a survey of the themes of aggression, action, feeding, denial, and omission are presented. No marked differences between the groups were obtained and no conclusions were drawn from this interim report.

Rabin, A. I. Infants and children under condition of intermittent mothering in the Kibbutz. *American Journal of Orthopsychiatry,* **1958, 28: 577–584.**

A group of twenty-four Kibbutz infants was compared on standard developmental scales with a group of twenty Moshav infants. On the vineland Social Maturity Scale and on the Griffiths Mental development scale the Kibbutz children tended to score below the Moshav children. A comparison of forty Kibbutz ten-year-olds with forty Moshav children of the same age on several measures of ego development (Goodenough, Rorschach) yielded data indicating the superiority of the Kibbutz group. The results are interpreted as indicating the transitoriness of the effects of the "intermittence" of mothering upon the development of the child in the Kibbutz.

Rapaport, D. The study of Kibbutz education and its bearing on the theory of development, *American Journal of Orthopsychiatry,* **1958, 28: 587–597.**

This theoretical article outlines the historical and ideological foundations of the Kibbutz movement and points out that "the Kibbutz movement arose as a rebellion against the religious, paternalistic-familial, socioeconomic and minority life of East European Jewry." Collective education has as its major aim the perpetuation of the Kibbutz and was motivated by the rebellion against patriarchal authority and dominance, against the pathology resulting from that authority, and against the institution of the bourgeois family.

After briefly reviewing the standard procedures in collective education Rapaport proposes several areas in which its effects have been particularly noted—interpersonal relationships, development of "problem" behavior and of personal effectiveness. These issues are discussed in the light of the limited information available. The paper ends with a plea for systematic studies to support or contradict the generalizations thus far drawn.

Segal, M. *Essays on education.* (Hebrew.) Tel-Aviv: Hakibbutz Hameuchad, 1955.

This collection of essays by one of the leaders and pioneers of the Kibbutz educational system, especially of the federation known as "Hakibbutz Hameuchad," spans a period of about twenty years. Most of them were previously published in different educational magazines and collections; some were not previously published. The essays are primarily theoretical statements and accounts of experimental approaches in collective education.

The volume is subdivided into five sections titled: Partnership in education, the theory of practice, day by day in school, the teachers seminary of the Kibbutzim, and "a time of change." In the first section the author attempts a detailed treatment of the comparison of Kibbutz with family childrearing. He points out that it was the children's house that was the original creation of Kibbutz childrearing and stresses the necessity for a "natural" age division in the houses. He sees particular advantage in the "extended kindergarten" ranging in ages from about two to over seven years. The wide spread in the ages is seen as possessing some of the advan-

108

tages of the family and is considered preferable to the strict peer group of a narrow age-range. An analysis of parent-child interaction and the integration of the child into the broader cultural setting of the Kibbutz is then presented. Particular stress is placed on the unconditional aspects of the love and relationships between parents and children.

In the second section the objection to the narrow-range peer groups crops up again:—"At the end of the second year most of the children have matured to an active and varie-gated environmental life—they are ready for the kindergar-ten. The toddlers house is not to be seen as such an environment. The toddlers by themselves are unable to main-tain a full environment. They need the richer initiative of five and six-year-olds." In addition, this section is concerned with the development of the social life among the children's units, the structure of the school and its relationship to youth movements, the daily life of the child, and the processes of learning in children.

The next section deals with the day by day activities in a small Kibbutz school system (in Kfar Gileadi). The daily program, physical work, educational outings and curricular issues are discussed. Children learning to work and the em-ployment of the children's educational farm for educational purposes as well as a consideration of group discussions are contained in this section.

In the remaining two sections, problems of educating teachers and educators and the desirable directions for the Kibbutz teachers seminary are outlined in some detail. Some of the educational goals stressed are: "a direct sense of na-ture, work culture and technology." Additional issues are treated, especially in the article authored in connection with the thirteenth anniversary of "Seminar Hakibbutzim".

Spiro, M.E. Education in a communal village in Israel. *American Journal of Orthopsychiatry*, 1955, 25, 283–292.

A preliminary ethnographic description of Kiryat Yedidim, a Kibbutz upon which the author's later major publications are based. Stress is placed on the psychological influences of the nurses, parents, and peers in the Kibbutz setting. The view is that "parents remain the crucial figures in the child's life." Also reported are some data (not in detail or tabular form) regarding responses of Kibbutz children, at several age levels, to the Bavelas Moral Ideology and Stewart Emotional Response tests. The "good things they could do," for which children would be praised, shows mainly concern with the approval of the "group" as compared with "parents" in other societies. Things for which they would be blamed involve the parental surrogates (nurses) most frequently in the younger age groups and the peer group at older age levels. "The influence of the peer group increases with age." Only about ten to thirteen percent of the children mention parents in connection with the "best thing" that could happen to them, compared with fifty per cent in the USA. Practically no family member was mentioned by Kibbutz children in response to "On what occasions have you been angry?", while fifty per cent of American subjects involve family members. The remainder of the paper deals with an evaluation of the educational system.

Vinograd, Marilyn. The development of the young child in a collective settlement. *American Journal of Orthopsychiatry*, 1958, 28: 557–562.

The author who had served as a *metapelet* for several years recorded detailed observations of a group of four-year-olds who were placed in her care. The description contains, in addition to a report of the behavior of the children, some observations concerning the relationship between them and their mothers. Special attention is given to an analysis of the role of the *metapelet* in the childrearing process and her relationship with the child's biological parents in the total Kibbutz setting.

Wollins, M. Group care: friend or foe. *Social Work,* **1969, 14: 35-53**

In the context of a more extensive report on the development of children in group settings in several cultures, some relevant data concerning Kibbutz children are also reported. A small sample (N=33) of Kibbutz children achieved the highest mean percentile on the Raven Progressive Matrices and differs from the others on five factors derived from a Value Inventory. The factors on which the Kibbutz group seems to be highest are: "other orientation," "controlled achievement," and "detachment." The general, overall conclusion of the article is that "children reared in five different types of group care programs appear to show little or no intellectual or psychosocial deficiencies when compared with controls from home environments."

Yarrow, L. J. Maternal deprivation: toward an empirical and conceptual re-evaluation. *Psychological Bulletin,* **1961, 58: 459–490.**

Within the context of a review of "four different kinds of deviation from a hypothetical mode of maternal care," the author discusses Kibbutz childrearing under the rubric of "multiple mothering." His conclusion is that "there is no clear evidence that multiple mothering, without associated deprivation or stress, results in personality damage."

Eisenstadt, S.N. *From generation to generation.* Glencoe,
Illinois: The Free Press, 1956.

Of major significance is the idea of discontinuity between
the world of adults (parents) and the younger generation in
the Kibbutz as compared with the Moshav, where "the
family constitutes the basic unit of agricultural production,
and agricultural familism constitutes one of its main ideals.
. . . There exists almost no discontinuity between the world
of the parents and that of the children. . . . The reverse is true
of the Kibbutz." The age groups and youth organizations in
the Kibbutz are of major social significance and exemplify
the discontinuity between the generations. The differences
are related to the differences in family and economic (production and consumption) structure of the two settings. Kibbutz adolescence is viewed as the period of preparation for
the adult communal life.

Friedmann, G. *The end of the Jewish people?* New York:
Anchor Books, 1968.

In the context of the larger volume there is one chapter
(no. 2) which deals exclusively with the Kibbutz and is entitled: "The Kibbutz Adventure and Challenges of the Century." In addition to some general background data and a
discussion of economic problems which the Kibbutz faces,
the author addresses himself to crucial social and psychological issues as well. He stresses the aspects of "a democratic
microsociety," the relatively important role of parents in
childrearing and the maintenance and even strengthening of

the family ties. He also concerns himself with the dangers of the relative segregation and isolation of the Kibbutzim from the "other society" and the possible effects of hostility from without. With respect to the future which is the major concern of this socio-economic, political, and psychological analysis it is concluded that "the *Kibbutz* will not survive in Israel unless it adapts itself to the economic and technical imperatives of profitability and productivity and at the same time preserves its driving force and essential standards and values, remaining all the time a myth, a living formative utopia."

Katz, F. Kibbutz children as parents. (Hebrew.)
Hachinuch Hameshutaft, **1964, 14: 3–7**

After surveying a sample of 400 young Kibbutz-born mothers in seventeen different Kibbutzim, the author feels that despite the great concern with the "problem of the woman" there is also a good deal of evidence concerning the satisfaction of the women generally, and with the educational system of the Kibbutz in particular. Some of the major conclusions are:

A. There is great stability in the female membership of the Kibbutz; the particularly serious defections are concentrated in a very small number of Kibbutzim.

B. The reasons for leaving the Kibbutz are not all due to the mother's attitude toward collective education. We found negative attitudes toward the children's house only in a few instances. This was an expression of a fundamentally negative attitude to the Kibbutz in general and towards its form of life.

C. About eighty-seven percent of these women see in the Kibbutz their way of life; thirteen per cent are conflicted. The

attitude toward collective education is positive in eighty percent, critical (but not negative) in seventeen per cent, and
definitely negative in three percent of the cases.

The general conclusion is that of general satisfaction of
Kibbutz women with the Kibbutz and their mothering functions in its setting.

Parsons, E.I. Children of Kfar Blum. *Midstream,* **1959, 5
(3); 64–75**

A member of a Kibbutz describes several aspects of Kibbutz life, especially those dealing with the younger generation. Most pertinent is a description of a rebellious-
"delinquent" group of adolescents, as well as comments
about the generation gap. Also of interest is the debate which
preceeded a Kibbutz vote concerned with children's sleeping
arrangements: whether children should continue in the children's house or be moved to rooms adjacent to parents'
quarters—an arrangement advocated by a minority of the
adult population. Arguments pro and con are outlined.

**Rettig, S. and Passamanick, B. Some observations on the
moral ideology of first and second generation collective
and non-collective settlers in Israel.** *Social Problems,*
1963, 11: 165–178.

Six hundred first and second generation settlers of Polish
descent, of collective and non-collective villages, were interviewed individually and asked to judge fifty morally disputable behaviors as to rightness or wrongness. The data were

factor-analyzed (yielding nine dimensions) and an analysis of variance was performed resulting in information on severity of judgment as a function of generational and collectivity differences and the interaction between them. Settlers of the collectives "were successful in transmitting and preserving a significantly different ideology in its second generation . . . deemphasis of religious and family moral standards, a heightened societal responsibility and national identity, a more severe rejection of exploitative practices and a greater stress of self-labor, increased aversion to injustice and cruelty, and a greater sanctity of human life. However, on one most fundamental dimension, mutual aid and trust, the collective settlers failed to instill in themselves higher standards." The failure was viewed as a result of the fact that the original settlers themselves were not reared in a collective. Recent institutional changes in the Kibbutz are also explained on the same basis.

Spiro, M.E. The sabras and Zionism: a study in personality and ideology. *Social Problems,* **1957, 5: 100–110.**

Based on his experience as a participant observer, the author concludes that the sabras (Israeli born) of the Kibbutz "lack an ideological basis which would justify the hardships and disabilities which are the lot of all Israelis; they are loathe to accept the Zionist premise of the national unity of the Jewish people, and therefore of the ingathering of the exiles." They also "assume that Judaism is an inferior culture." The basis for their Zionism is economic progress, self defense, and self preservation. This state of affairs is related, by the author, to the hostility felt by the sabras, which in turn is seen as a defense against feelings of shame and inferiority resulting from a negatively valued identification.

Talmon-Garber, Y. Young and old in the Israeli Kibbutzim. (French.) *Esprit,* **1963, 31 (6): 952–964.**

"Sources of tension" between the younger generation in the Kibbutz and the older generation are detailed. Special attention is paid to those aspects of the original principles of Kibbutz ideology (importance of work, physical strength, etc.) which place the aging and aged individual at a disadvantage.

Some social and economic "solutions" or adjustments are proposed. These include the progressive reduction of work hours, reorganization of existing occupational activities, and the introduction of innovations to facilitate the work of the aged. Also, they include introduction of some aged to appropriate work outside the Kibbutz, giving further opportunities for adult education and the facilitation of their participation in the social and internal life of the community. Finally, the creation of an institution for the aged infirm is considered ultimately as a realistic necessity.

XI.   BIBLIOGRAPHIES

Cohen, E. *Bibliography of the Kibbutz.* **Givat Haviva, Israel: 1964.**

A wide variety of references in several languages are listed, ranging between 1945 and 1964, in this compilation undertaken at the Sociology Department of the Hebrew University. The subtitle of the pamphlet indicates that it is "A selection of recent sociological and related publications on collective settlements in European languages." The list of references contains systematic studies as well as descriptive accounts and polemics regarding various aspects of Kibbutz life and ideology. Bibliographic items are classified under the following rubrics: (1) general, (2) history of the Kibbutz movement, (3) federations of Kibbutzim, (4) particular communities, (5) demography, (6) political and organizational structure, (7) economy, (8) working process, (9) consumption, (10) culture and recreation, (11) stratification, (12) family age and sex, (13) education, socialization and mental development, (14) second generation, and (15) miscellaneous.

Horigan, Francis D. The Israeli Kibbutz (psychiatric, psychological, and social studies with emphasis on family life and family structure). *Psychiatric Abstracts Series No. 9.* **National Institutes of Health, Bethesda, Md., 1962.**

A 100-item bibliography, one half of which is abstracted, may be found in this publication. Hebrew as well as English sources are listed. A few references in other languages may be found. Not all the items, however, are directly related to the Kibbutz. Some of them deal with broader issues of education and Israeli youth in general. It is nevertheless a useful document in which most of the relevant literature prior to 1962 is covered.

Shatil, J. *Bibliography (Temporary) of Studies of Rural Cooperation in Israel.* **Jerusalem: State of Israel; Ministry of Labor, 1965 (Mimeo), 46 pp.**

This publication is a classified list of references (mainly to Hebrew sources) in several languages concerning the Kibbutzim and Moshavim (old and new) in Israel. The classification is represented by the following eight categories of bibliographic items: 1. General, history, statistics, population, etc.; 2. Economy, finance; 3. Farm management; 4. Sociology; 5. Organization, administration, law; 6. Culture, education, ideology; 7. Regional cooperation, village planning; and 8. Rural industry. Under each heading the items are further placed under the following rubrics: rural cooperation in general, Kibbutz and Kvutzah, Moshav, new Moshavim, and other types of rural cooperation.

Although many references are in English, French, German, etc., the bulk of the references is in Hebrew, and to many "internal" publications or mimeographed surveys or reports. Also, a large percentage of the items consists of rather specialized surveys of limited scope and of essays about various aspects of Kibbutz life.

Shur, S. *Kibbutz bibliography.* **Jerusalem, Tel-Aviv and Givat Haviva: 1970.**

In this provisional extension and updating of Cohen's 1964 bibliography, the editor-compiler attempts to "approach a complete (not selective) bibliography that will include everything written on the Kibbutz in languages other than Hebrew." Upward of 700 references are included in this pamphlet. A large proportion of these are non-technical descriptive, polemic, and editorial pieces that appeared in such publications as "Israel Horizons," "Jewish Frontier" and other labor-Zionist organs. However, nearly all available non-Hebrew professional and scientific references are also included and categorized.

GLOSSARY

Hashomer Hatzair—(literal translation: the young guard)—youth organization which furnished (and still does) recruits for the Kibbutz movement. It is affiliated with the Kibbutz Artzi federation

Ichud (literally: union)—one of the federations of Kvutzot and Kibbutzim affiliated with the moderate socialist party "Mapai"

Kibbutz (pl., Kibbutzim)—communal settlement in Israel (literal meaning-meeting or gathering)

Kibbutznik—a member of a Kibbutz

Knesset—Israel's parliament

Kvutzah (pl., Kvutzoth)—term used in two ways: 1. a small Kibbutz, especially characteristic of the early period of the Kibbutz movement; 2. a group of four to six children who live together as a unit in the children's house; the group is usually increased in size after the pre-school years

Kibbutz Artzi—the largest federation in the Kibbutz movement, affiliated with the leftist "Mapam" party

Kibbutz Menchad—one of the three largest federations of Kibbutizim, located politically between the Ichud and the Kibbutz Artzi.

Mechanech—educator, counselor, and guide of school-age children

Metapelet (pl., metaplot; literally; caretaker)—infant nurse and/or housemother in the children's houses of the system of collective education

121

Mosad—junior and senior high school-level institute

Moshav (pl., Moshavim)—cooperative settlement in Israel; primarily cooperative economically (joint consumer and marketing cooperative)

Moshava (pl., moshavot)—conventional village inhabited entirely by private land owners

Sabra—native born Israeli

Seminar Hakibbutzim—training college for teachers, metaplot and other educators—established and run by the Kibbutz movement

Shtetl—small town in Eastern Europe

Index of Authors

123